OFFICIAL SQA PAST PAPERS
WITH ANSWERS

STANDARD GRADE | FOUNDATION | GENERAL | CREDIT

DRAMA
2006-2010

First exam published in 2006.
Published by Bright Red Publishing Ltd, 6 Stafford Street, Edinburgh EH3 7AU
tel: 0131 220 5804 fax: 0131 220 6710 info@brightredpublishing.co.uk www.brightredpublishing.co.uk

ISBN 978-1-84948-086-4

A CIP Catalogue record for this book is available from the British Library.

Bright Red Publishing is grateful to the copyright holders, as credited on the final page of the book, for permission to use their material. Every effort has been made to trace the copyright holders and to obtain their permission for the use of copyright material. Bright Red Publishing will be happy to receive information allowing us to rectify any error or omission in future editions.

STANDARD GRADE | FOUNDATION | GENERAL | CREDIT

2006

[BLANK PAGE]

F G C

0700/404

NATIONAL
QUALIFICATIONS
2006

FRIDAY, 19 MAY
F:　9.00 AM – 9.45 AM
G: 10.05 AM – 10.50 AM
C: 11.10 AM – 12.10 PM

DRAMA
STANDARD GRADE
Foundation, General
and Credit Levels
Stimulus Paper

Study carefully the five stimuli (i), (ii), (iii), (iv) and (v) before answering the questions in Section A of the Question Paper.

SCOTTISH
QUALIFICATIONS
AUTHORITY

　©

STIMULUS (i)

Truth and Consequences

STIMULUS (ii)

STIMULUS (iii)

As cold as ice
As sharp as a knife
As dead as a doornail

STIMULUS (iv)

Call for Help

The following items were found by a jogger in Homestead Park on Tuesday evening: a mobile phone, a gold watch and an old black and white photograph of a young child. Anyone who thinks they may be able to assist police with their enquiries is requested to contact their local police station.

[Turn over for Stimulus (v) on *Page four*

STIMULUS (v)

TANYA: . . . I went downstairs and outside with the rubbish. It was going to be a lovely day. Blossom on the trees. Spring flowers in the garden. I thought I might pick some and leave them on the table for Stefan to see when he came in. The sun was up in the air. It's hard to explain. At first I thought there had been a frost in the night but it was too warm for frost. There was a little garden outside the block of flats and they had planted roses. The new glossy leaves had this fine white powder on them. Like ash. I touched it. Something else. No birds were singing. None at all . . .

Extract from *Wormwood* by Catherine Czerkawska

[END OF STIMULUS PAPER]

FOR OFFICIAL USE

F

Total

0700/401

NATIONAL
QUALIFICATIONS
2006

FRIDAY, 19 MAY
9.00 AM – 9.45 AM

DRAMA
STANDARD GRADE
Foundation Level

Fill in these boxes and read what is printed below.

Full name of centre

Town

Forename(s)

Surname

Date of birth

Day   Month   Year   Scottish candidate number   Number of seat

1   Read each question carefully.

2   Attempt **all** questions in **both** sections.

3   You may use sketches and diagrams to illustrate your answers.

4   All answers are to be written in this answer book. If there is not enough space for you to complete your answer to any question, **additional paper** can be obtained from the invigilator.

5   The Stimuli for Section A are supplied in a separate paper. Check that you have this paper before the examination begins.

6   Before leaving the examination room you must give this book to the invigilator. If you do not, you may lose all the marks for this paper.

SCOTTISH
QUALIFICATIONS
AUTHORITY

SA 0700/401 6/4670

Marks

SECTION A

Answer **all** of the following questions.

> Your answers should be based
> on work from the **stimulus material**.
> (*A copy of the Stimulus Paper is provided.*)

My group chose stimulus _____ (*enter number from Stimulus Paper*).

1. Use the space below to write a **brief scenario** of the drama created by your group.

A **brief** summary of the action	
Beginning	
Middle	
End	

6

Marks

2.   Complete the following Character Card for **your character.**

Full name and age: _____   1

Occupation: _____   1

Personality: _____

_____

_____

_____   2

Appearance (eg height, build, style of dress): _____

_____

_____

_____   2

Other information about your character: _____

_____

_____

_____   1

[Turn over

DO NOT
WRITE IN
THIS MARGIN

Marks

3. (*a*) What was the **most important moment** in your drama for **your character**?

_____

_____

_____   1

(*b*) Why was this moment important?

_____

_____

_____   1

(*c*) Describe how your character **spoke** at that moment.

_____

_____

_____

_____   2

(*d*) Describe how your character **moved** at that moment.

_____

_____

_____

_____   2

(*e*) Theatre Arts are:

Lighting	Sound	Props	Set	Costume	Make-up

In what ways would you use **one** of these at this important moment in your drama?

_____

_____   1

Marks

4. In the space below draw a ground plan of the acting area for **one** scene of your drama.

This scene takes place in _____

Key:

5

DO NOT
WRITE IN
THIS MARGIN

Marks

SECTION B

Answer **all** of the following questions.

> Your answers should **not** be based
> on work from the **stimulus material**.

5. Read the following questions and put a tick (✓) in the box next to the correct answer.

(a) A drama presented through dance moves is a

mime ☐
dance drama ☐
monologue ☐
convention ☐

(b) The speed of movement or speech is called

body language ☐
volume ☐
height ☐
pace ☐

(c) The final rehearsal of a play with all theatre arts is a

dress rehearsal ☐
presentation ☐
technical rehearsal ☐
practice ☐

(d) The outline of the plot of a drama is called a

script ☐
scenario ☐
story ☐
convention ☐

(e) The build up of excitement in a drama is called

timing ☐
acting ☐
tension ☐
plot ☐

(f) The signal for an actor to say or do something is

dramatic moment ☐
mime ☐
sign ☐
cue ☐

(g) When a character shakes a fist they use a

role-play ☐
point ☐
signal ☐
gesture ☐

7

Marks

6. Look carefully at the two characters in the picture below.

Then answer questions (*a*) to (*h*) which follow.

Read all the questions before starting to write.

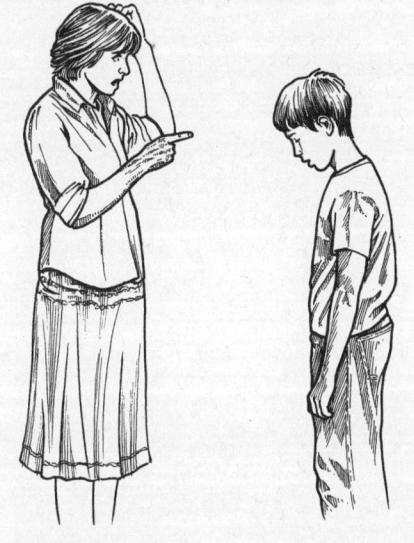

Character A   Character B

They are two characters in a drama.

(*a*) Who is character A?

_____   1

(*b*) Who is character B?

_____   1

(*c*) What do you see **happening** in this picture?

_____

_____

_____   2

(*d*) **When** and **where** is this happening?

_____

_____   1

(*e*) What do you think happened **before** this?

_____

_____

_____   2

[Turn over for Questions 6 (continued) and 7 on *Page eight*

Marks

6. **(continued)**

(*f*) How do you think character A is feeling?

_____   1

(*g*) How do you think character B is feeling?

_____   1

(*h*) What do you think happens next?

_____

_____

_____

_____

_____

_____

_____

_____   3

7. Look at the words below and write them in the correct column.

**musical   flashback   slow motion
pantomime   play   freeze frame**

Drama Form	Drama Convention

6

[*END OF QUESTION PAPER*]

FOR OFFICIAL USE

G

Total

0700/402

NATIONAL
QUALIFICATIONS
2006

FRIDAY, 19 MAY
10.05 AM – 10.50 AM

DRAMA
STANDARD GRADE
General Level

Fill in these boxes and read what is printed below.

Full name of centre

Town

Forename(s)

Surname

Date of birth
Day Month Year   Scottish candidate number   Number of seat

Read each question carefully.

Attempt **all** questions.

Write your answers in the space provided on the question paper.

Write as neatly as possible.

Answer in sentences wherever possible.

Before leaving the examination room you must give this book to the invigilator. If you do not, you may lose all the marks for this paper.

SCOTTISH
QUALIFICATIONS
AUTHORITY

©

Marks

SECTION A

Answer **all** of the following questions.

Your answers should be based
on work from the **stimulus material**.
(*A copy of the Stimulus Paper is provided.*)

My group chose stimulus _____ (*enter number from stimulus paper*).

1. Use the space below to write a **brief scenario** of the drama created by your group.

Scene number	Time, place and action

6

Marks

2.   (*a*)   List **three** characters in the drama including your own.

Give the role of each.

Your character _____

Role _____

Character 2 _____

Role _____

Character 3 _____

Role _____   **3**

(*b*)   Look at the list above. Describe the relationship between **your character** and character 2 **or** character 3.

_____

_____

_____

_____   **2**

(*c*)   Describe in what ways voice and movement were used to show this relationship.

_____

_____

_____

_____

_____   **3**

[Turn over

Marks

3.   Complete the following for a character played by **another member of your group**.

Full Name: _____ Age: _____   1

Occupation: _____   1

Physical Description: _____

_____

_____   2

Personality: _____

_____

_____   2

Costume: _____

_____

_____   3

Personal props: _____

_____

_____   3

4.

> **You have developed your drama from**
>
> **stimulus ⟶ final evaluation.**

What challenges did you and your group face during this process and how did you deal with them?

_____

_____

_____

_____

_____

_____

_____

_____

_____

4

[Turn over

SECTION B

Answer **all** of the following questions.

> Your answers should **not** be based on work from the
> **stimulus material**.

5. Read the following scenario.

    Scene 1   In a supermarket 11.30 pm.
    Danny is being led away by the police.
    His friends are cheering and Danny could not care less.

    Scene 2   Outside court building 10.30 am the next day.
    Danny walks down the steps to be met by his mother.
    His friends are not there.

    Describe Danny's **voice and movement** in each scene.

    Scene 1 _____

    _____

    _____

    _____

    _____

    _____

    _____

    _____   5

    Scene 2 _____

    _____

    _____

    _____

    _____

    _____

    _____

    _____   5

DO NOT
WRITE IN
THIS MARGIN

Marks

6. Explain what is meant by the drama term *Mime*.

Mime is _____   2

Now complete the words below.

To be effectively performed, *mime* should be:

S _____   1

P _____   1

E _____   1

C _____   1

S _____   1

7. Complete the grid below by adding in the correct **areas of the stage**.

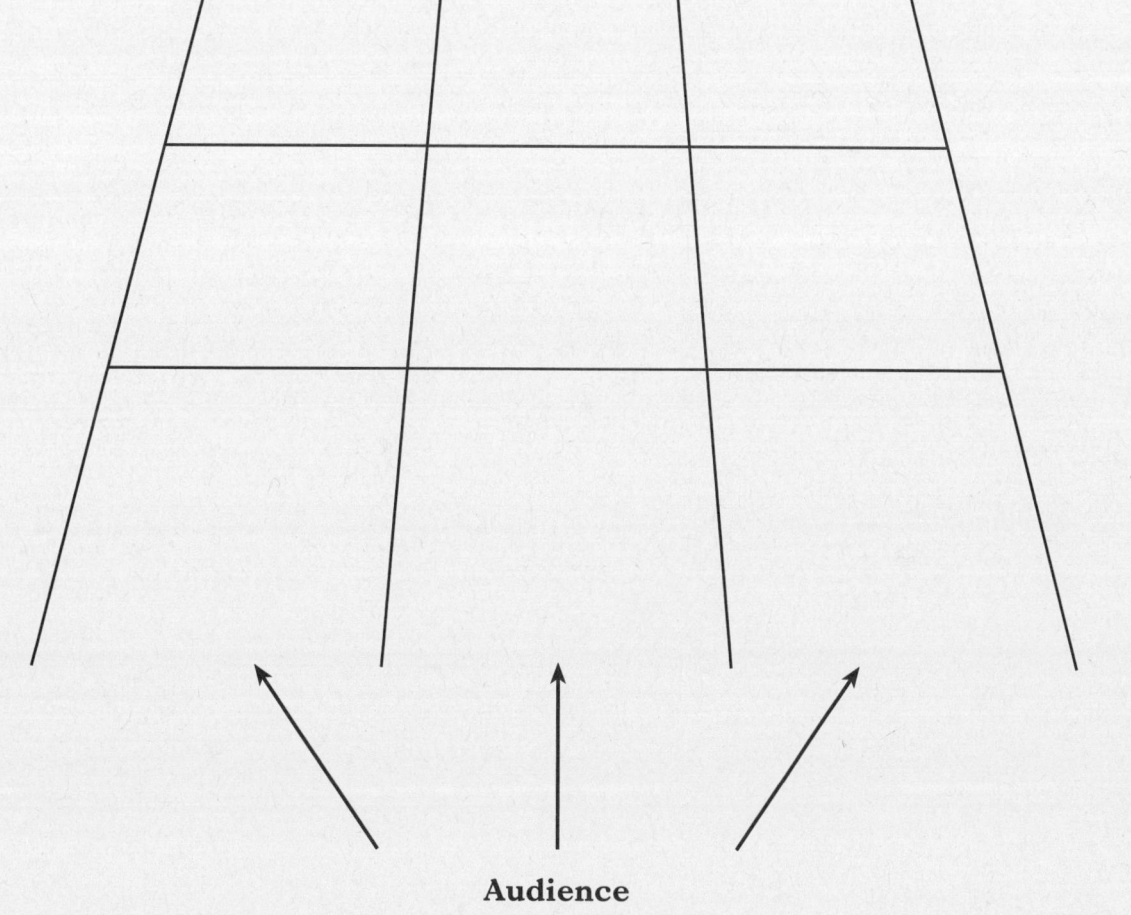

Audience

3

Marks

8.

Emily Carruthers, 72, sits alone in her favourite chair. She is leafing through her photograph album.

This is the start of a drama. Describe the set/set dressings, lighting and sound to accompany this opening stage picture.

Set/set dressings _____

_____

_____

_____

_____

_____

_____

_____

4

Lighting _____

_____

_____

_____

_____

3

DO NOT
WRITE IN
THIS MARGIN

Marks

8.   **(continued)**

Sound _____

_____

_____

_____

_____

_____   **3**

[*END OF QUESTION PAPER*]

[BLANK PAGE]

FOR OFFICIAL USE

C

Total

0700/403

NATIONAL
QUALIFICATIONS
2006

FRIDAY, 19 MAY
11.10 AM – 12.10 PM

DRAMA
STANDARD GRADE
Credit Level

Fill in these boxes and read what is printed below.

Full name of centre

Town

Forename(s)

Surname

Date of birth
  Day Month Year   Scottish candidate number   Number of seat

1 Read each question carefully.

2 Attempt **all** questions in **both** sections.

3 You may use sketches and diagrams to illustrate your answers.

4 All answers are to be written in this answer book. If there is not enough space for you to complete your answer to any question, **additional paper** can be obtained from the invigilator.

5 The Stimuli for Section A are supplied in a separate paper. Check that you have this paper before the examination begins.

6 Before leaving the examination room you must give this book to the invigilator. If you do not, you may lose all the marks for this paper.

SCOTTISH
QUALIFICATIONS
AUTHORITY

SECTION A

Answer **all** of the following questions.

Marks

> Your answers should be based
> on work from the **stimulus material**.
> (*A copy of the Stimulus Paper is provided.*)

My group chose stimulus _____ (*enter number from Stimulus Paper*).

"The purpose of a drama must be established in order to communicate a meaning."

1. (*a*) What was the purpose of your drama?

_____   1

   (*b*) Did your drama achieve this purpose? How did you know?

_____

_____

_____

_____

_____   2

2. (*a*) Which part of the plot do you feel was communicated most effectively?

_____

_____   1

   (*b*) Explain why this was the case.

_____

_____

_____

_____

_____

_____

_____   3

Marks

3.   (*a*)   Which **character** was, in your opinion, portrayed most successfully?

_____

1

   (*b*)   Explain how the **actor** achieved this.

_____

_____

_____

_____

_____

_____

_____

_____

_____

_____

4

[Turn over

4. How could you have used theatre arts to enhance two key moments in your drama? Use a different theatre art for each moment and justify your answer.

Moment 1 _____

_____

_____

_____

_____

_____

_____

_____

4

Moment 2 _____

_____

_____

_____

_____

_____

_____

_____

4

DO NOT
WRITE IN
THIS MARGIN

Marks

SECTION B

Answer **all** of the following questions.

> Your answers should **not** be based
> on work from the **stimulus material**.

5. *"Tension is the driving force of a drama."*

   (a) List **five** ways in which tension can be created.

       1 _____

       2 _____

       3 _____

       4 _____

       5 _____   5

   (b) Explain how Dramatic Tension was used in a drama in which you took part
       during your Standard Grade Drama Course.
       You may wish to expand on, or add to, your answer to 5 (a).

       _____

       _____

       _____

       _____

       _____

       _____

       _____

       _____

       _____

       _____

       _____

       _____   8

                                                         [Turn over

Marks

6. Write the correct word after each definition.

(a) Appropriate speech for the person being spoken to. _____

(b) Audience seated on two sides of the acting area. _____

(c) To remove all the set from the acting area. _____

(d) One actor unintentionally preventing
another from being seen by the audience. _____

(e) Lantern giving a hard edged beam of light. _____   **5**

7.

Name **five** items of stage make-up needed to create this character of a tramp.

1 _____

2 _____

3 _____

4 _____

5 _____   **5**

DO NOT
WRITE IN
THIS MARGIN

Marks

8. Imagine that your group has been asked to devise a drama entitled

"World in Danger"

(*a*) Write a scenario of a drama, suitable for acting out.
Include time, place and key characters/relationships.

_____

_____

_____

_____

_____

_____

_____

_____

_____

_____

_____

_____

_____

_____

_____

_____

_____

_____

8

8. (continued)

(b) Think of the overall style or design concepts for your drama.
Describe in what ways **set** and **costume** would add to the overall effect you wish to communicate to your audience.

7

Marks

8.   (continued)

(*c*) Describe what you consider to be the climax or key event in your drama.
Say why.

_____

_____

_____

_____

_____   2

(*d*) Imagine this moment as a **tableau**. Describe how it would look.

_____

_____

_____

_____

_____

_____

_____

_____

_____

_____   4

[Turn over

8. **(continued)**

(*e*) Choose **two** from the following list. Describe how you might use them and how each would enhance the impact of the tableau.

Use of levels   **SFX**   **Props**   **Voice-over**   **LFX**

_____

_____

_____

_____

_____

_____

_____

_____

_____

_____

_____

_____

_____

_____   6

[*END OF QUESTION PAPER*]

STANDARD GRADE | FOUNDATION | GENERAL | CREDIT

2007

[BLANK PAGE]

F G C

0700/404

NATIONAL
QUALIFICATIONS
2007

TUESDAY, 15 MAY
F: 9.00 AM – 9.45 AM
G: 10.05 AM – 10.50 AM
C: 11.10 AM – 12.10 PM

**DRAMA
STANDARD GRADE**
Foundation, General
and Credit Levels
Stimulus Paper

Study carefully the five stimuli (i), (ii), (iii), (iv) and (v)
before answering the questions in Section A of the
Question Paper.

SCOTTISH
QUALIFICATIONS
AUTHORITY

©

STIMULUS (i)

Confessed faults are half mended.

Scottish Proverb

STIMULUS (ii)

Flight
Quint Buchholz

STIMULUS (iii)

Like curs a glance has brought to heel, . . .
We listen'd flinching there:
And look'd, and look'd, on the untouched meal
And the overtoppled chair.

Wilfred Wilson Gibson (Flannan Isle)

STIMULUS (iv)

1. **neb**: Another word for nose: "Jist you keep yer neb oot o' this."

(Scots Dictionary)

[Turn over for Stimulus (v) on *Page four*

STIMULUS (v)

ONCE IN A LIFETIME OPPORTUNITY!

Generate a substantial income and build yourself a worthwhile pension. Part time/full time involvement in an ethical, reputable and proven marketing campaign in preventative medicine. Moderate outlay (5/20K + VAT)

For details ring Freephone 0800 555 1212

Companion Wanted

To share car and help pay fuel.

Leaving for London soon.

TELEPHONE PROFITS

* Horoscope * Tarot *

You are paid
for every call received.
No equipment required
No training required

Dreams can come true

FOR SALE

Wedding dress (white) size 14. Never worn.

[END OF STIMULUS PAPER]

FOR OFFICIAL USE

F

Total

0700/401

NATIONAL
QUALIFICATIONS
2007

TUESDAY, 15 MAY
9.00 AM – 9.45 AM

DRAMA
STANDARD GRADE
Foundation Level

Fill in these boxes and read what is printed below.

Full name of centre

Town

Forename(s)

Surname

Date of birth

Day Month Year   Scottish candidate number   Number of seat

1 Read each question carefully.

2 Attempt **all** questions in **both** sections.

3 You may use sketches and diagrams to illustrate your answers.

4 All answers are to be written in this answer book. If there is not enough space for you to complete your answer to any question, **additional paper** can be obtained from the invigilator.

5 The Stimuli for Section A are supplied in a separate paper. Check that you have this paper before the examination begins.

6 Before leaving the examination room you must give this book to the invigilator. If you do not, you may lose all the marks for this paper.

SCOTTISH
QUALIFICATIONS
AUTHORITY

©

SECTION A

Answer **all** of the following questions.

> Your answers should be based
> on work from the **stimulus material**.
> (*A copy of the Stimulus Paper is provided.*)

My group chose stimulus _____ (*enter number from Stimulus Paper*).

1. Think back to the story of the drama created by your group.

   (*a*) What happened at the beginning of your drama?

   3

   (*b*) What happened at the end of your drama?

   3

DO NOT
WRITE IN
THIS MARGIN

Marks

2. Complete the following Character Card for **your character.**

Full name and age: _____   1

Occupation: _____   1

Appearance: _____

_____

_____

_____   3

Name **two** items of costume for your character:

_____

_____   2

Name **one** personal prop for your character:

_____   1

[Turn over

DO NOT
WRITE IN
THIS MARG

Marks

3. Read all of the parts of this question before you start to write.

Think back to the drama created by your group.

(*a*) Which part of the action was the most dramatic?

_____

_____   1

(*b*) Give a reason for your answer.

_____

_____   1

(*c*) Name a character in that part of the action.

_____   1

(*d*) How did that character **speak** in that part of the action?

_____

_____

_____   2

(*e*) How did that character **move** in that part of the action?

_____

_____

_____   2

3.   (continued)

Marks

(f) Theatre arts are:

Lighting	Sound	Props	Set	Costume	Make-up

Choose two of these you would like to use at this dramatic part of the action.

This is how I would use them and why:

Theatre art 1

_____

_____

_____

2

Theatre art 2

_____

_____

_____

2

[Turn over

SECTION B

Answer **all** of the following questions.

Your answers should **not** be based
on work from the **stimulus material**.

4. Here is a ground plan.

   Look at it carefully and answer the questions on the opposite page.

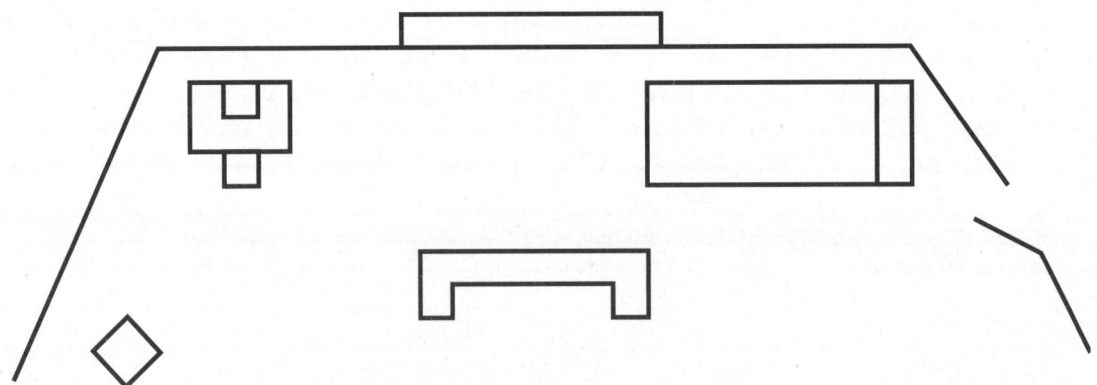

Audience

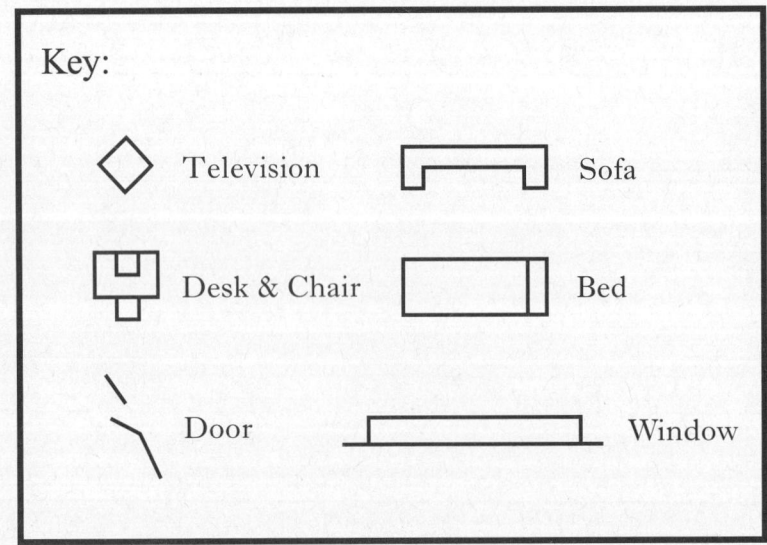

4.   (continued)

Marks

(*a*)   The door is
(Tick (✓) **one** box.)

☐ USR
☐ DSR
☐ CSL

1

(*b*)   The sofa is
(Tick (✓) **one** box.)

☐ USL
☐ CSR
☐ CS

1

(*c*)   The desk and chair are
(Tick (✓) **one** box.)

☐ USR
☐ DSL
☐ CSR

1

(*d*)   Where is the television? _____

1

(*e*)   Where is the bed? _____

1

(*f*)   Where is the window? _____

1

[Turn over

DO NOT
WRITE IN
THIS MARGIN

Marks

5. Imagine this is the opening scene of a drama.

A public park.
It is sunny and hot.

This is a drawing of the set.

Two characters are about to enter.

(*a*) Who might they be?

Character 1 _____

Character 2 _____   **2**

(*b*) Why might they be there?

Character 1 (*reason*) _____

_____

Character 2 (*reason*) _____

_____   **2**

(*c*) In what two ways would you like to **light** this scene, and why?

1 _____

Reason _____

2 _____

Reason _____   **4**

DO NOT
WRITE IN
THIS MARGIN

Marks

5.   (continued)

(*d*) In what two ways would you like to use **sound** in this scene, and why?

1 _____

Reason _____

2 _____

Reason _____

4

[Turn over for Question 6 on *Page ten*

Marks

6. Write the correct word(s) in the space provided.

(a) A drama which includes song and/or music is a _____

1

(b) The people watching a drama are called the _____

1

(c) Clothes worn by actors for their character are called _____

1

(d) To leave the acting area is to _____

1

(e) Blocks or platforms used to create levels are called _____

1

(f) A stage with the audience seated on three sides of the acting area is called

_____

1

(g) Movement performed at a slowed down speed is called _____

1

[END OF QUESTION PAPER]

FOR OFFICIAL USE

G

Total

0700/402

NATIONAL	TUESDAY, 15 MAY	DRAMA
QUALIFICATIONS	10.05 AM – 10.50 AM	STANDARD GRADE
2007		General Level

Fill in these boxes and read what is printed below.

Full name of centre

Town

Forename(s)

Surname

Date of birth

Day Month Year   Scottish candidate number   Number of seat

1 Read each question carefully.

2 Attempt **all** questions in **both** sections.

3 You may use sketches and diagrams to illustrate your answers.

4 All answers are to be written in this answer book. If there is not enough space for you to complete your answer to any question, **additional paper** can be obtained from the invigilator.

5 The Stimuli for Section A are supplied in a separate paper. Check that you have this paper before the examination begins.

6 Before leaving the examination room you must give this book to the invigilator. If you do not, you may lose all the marks for this paper.

SCOTTISH
QUALIFICATIONS
AUTHORITY

SA 0700/402 6/9770   ©

Marks

SECTION A

Answer **all** of the following questions.

┌───┐
│   Your answers should be based   │
│   on work from the **stimulus material**.   │
│   (*A copy of the Stimulus Paper is provided.*)   │
└───┘

My group chose stimulus _____ (*enter number from stimulus paper*).

1. Use the space below to write a **brief scenario** of the drama created by your group.

Scene number	Time, place and action

6

DO NOT
WRITE IN
THIS MARGIN

Marks

2. (*a*) What was your character's **role** in the drama?

_____   1

(*b*) What was the most important moment in the drama for your character?

_____   1

(*c*) Why was this the most important moment for your character?

_____   1

3. Think of another character present at that moment.

Complete the following Character Card for that other character.

Full Name: _____ Age: _____   1

Occupation: _____   1

Physical Description: _____

_____

_____   2

Personality: _____

_____

_____

_____   3

4. Describe the relationship between your character and any other character in your drama. Give reasons for that relationship.

_____

_____

_____

_____   3

DO NOT
WRITE IN
THIS MARGIN

Marks

5. Think back to your group's drama.

In what ways would you have liked to use **two** of the following to enhance your drama and why?

lighting	**voice over**	**flashback**	**SFX**
	freeze frame	**music**	

_____

_____

_____

_____

_____

_____

_____

_____

6

DO NOT
WRITE IN
THIS MARGIN

Marks

6. Look at the following voice words. Select **five** and say when they were used in your group's drama.

clarity   accent   emphasis   volume   pause   pitch   tone

(*a*) _____ was used when _____

_____ 1

(*b*) _____ was used when _____

_____ 1

(*c*) _____ was used when _____

_____ 1

(*d*) _____ was used when _____

_____ 1

(*e*) _____ was used when _____

_____ 1

[Turn over

DO NOT
WRITE IN
THIS MARGIN

Marks

SECTION B

Answer **all** of the following questions.

> Your answers should **not** be based on work from the **stimulus material**.

7.   Give the correct drama term for the following definitions.

Insert your answers in the spaces provided below.

(i) This person tells part(s) of the drama_____   1

(ii) A lantern giving a hard-edged beam of light_____   1

(iii) Change of voice to express emotion_____   1

(iv) Keeping an even distribution of weight _____   1

(v) Place where a drama is presented_____   1

(vi) The written words of a drama_____   1

Marks

8.   Read the following script then answer the questions below.

      A: **You've got to help me!**
      B: **Why should I?**
      A: **You can't mean that. After all I've done for you.**
      B: **Oh, I might have known you'd bring that up.**
      A: **Please.   I'm desperate.**
      B: **Well . . .**

(*a*)   Who are the characters?

_____

_____   2

(*b*)   **"Oh, I might have known you'd bring that up".** What do you think has happened between these two characters in the past?

_____

_____

_____

_____

_____   3

(*c*)   Which of the two characters do you think has the higher status and why?

_____

_____

_____

_____

_____   3

[Turn over

DO NOT
WRITE IN
THIS MARGIN

Marks

8. **(continued)**

(*d*) In what ways could facial expression, body language and gesture be used to show the status of **both** characters?

Facial expression _____

_____

_____

_____   **3**

Body language _____

_____

_____

_____   **3**

Gesture _____

_____

_____

_____   **3**

DO NOT
WRITE IN
THIS MARGIN

Marks

9. The diagrams below are of three different types of staging.

(a)

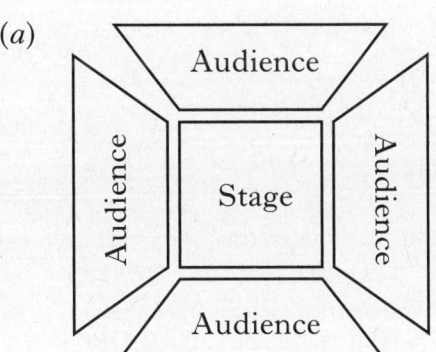

(b)

Stage

Audience

(c)

Stage   Audience

Name each type of staging.

(a) _____ 1

(b) _____ 1

(c) _____ 1

[Turn over for Question 10 on *Page ten*

DO NOT
WRITE IN
THIS MARGIN

Marks

10.   **"A variety of techniques can be used in the investigation of characterisation."**

In the list below are four of these characterisation techniques.

Identify the **four** by ticking the correct boxes.

1.	Posture	☐
2.	Hot-seating	☐
3.	Eye contact	☐
4.	Timing	☐
5.	Conflict	☐
6.	Voices in the head	☐
7.	Explore	☐
8.	Writing in role	☐
9.	Character cards	☐

4

[END OF QUESTION PAPER]

FOR OFFICIAL USE

C

Total ☐

0700/403

NATIONAL QUALIFICATIONS 2007

TUESDAY, 15 MAY 11.10 AM – 12.10 PM

DRAMA
STANDARD GRADE
Credit Level

Fill in these boxes and read what is printed below.

Full name of centre

Town

Forename(s)

Surname

Date of birth

Day Month Year   Scottish candidate number   Number of seat

1 Read each question carefully.

2 Attempt **all** questions in **both** sections.

3 You may use sketches and diagrams to illustrate your answers.

4 All answers are to be written in this answer book. If there is not enough space for you to complete your answer to any question, **additional paper** can be obtained from the invigilator.

5 The Stimuli for Section A are supplied in a separate paper. Check that you have this paper before the examination begins.

6 Before leaving the examination room you must give this book to the invigilator. If you do not, you may lose all the marks for this paper.

SCOTTISH
QUALIFICATIONS
AUTHORITY

©

Marks

SECTION A

Answer **all** of the following questions.

> Your answers should be based
> on work from the **stimulus material**.
> (*A copy of the Stimulus Paper is provided.*)

My group chose stimulus _____ (*enter number from Stimulus Paper*).

1.　(*a*)　Identify the central character in your drama.

Name _____ Age _____　**1**

(*b*)　Why was this character central to the drama?

_____

_____

_____

_____　**3**

(*c*)　Now think about the other characters in your drama. Choose any **two** and explain their purpose in the drama.

_____

_____

_____

_____

_____

_____　**4**

DO NOT
WRITE IN
THIS MARGIN

Marks

2. Think about the purpose or message of your drama. How did the plot help to communicate this purpose or message?

_____

_____

_____

_____

_____

_____

_____

_____

6

3. (a) What aspect of your presented drama had the greatest impact on your audience and why?

_____

_____

_____

2

(b) In what ways could theatre arts enhance this impact?

_____

_____

_____

_____

_____

_____

_____

4

[Turn over

Marks

SECTION B

Answer **all** of the following questions.

> Your answers should **not** be based
> on work from the **stimulus material**.

4. Give the definitions of the following drama terms.

(*a*) Barn doors _____

_____ 2

(*b*) Blocking _____

_____ 2

(*c*) Cyclorama _____

_____ 2

(*d*) Intonation _____

_____ 2

(*e*) Wings _____

_____ 2

Marks

5. This question requires an imaginative response from you.

Read carefully all parts of the question, (*a*) to (*e*), before starting to write.

> *A wild Scottish moor.*
> *Thunder and lightning.*
> *Night.*
> *Enter three characters.*

(*a*) Describe the mood and atmosphere you would wish to create at the start of the drama.

_____

(*b*) How could this mood and atmosphere be created through what the audience **sees** before the characters enter?

_____

_____

_____

_____

_____

_____   **4**

(*c*) How could this mood and atmosphere be created through what the audience **hears** before the characters enter?

_____

_____

_____

_____

_____

_____   **4**

[Turn over

5. (continued)

(d) How could this mood and atmosphere be created through the ways in which the three characters make their entrance?

_____

_____

_____

_____

_____

_____

_____

_____

4

(e) Describe how the three characters might look. Your answer must refer to physical description, make-up and costume. You may also include other visual information.

_____

_____

_____

_____

_____

_____

_____

_____

_____

_____

_____

_____

_____

_____

_____

_____

10

Marks

6.   Identify the following ground plan symbols.

(*a*)   ∼∼∼∼∼∼∼   _____   1

(*b*)   _____   1

(*c*)   _____   1

(*d*)   _____   1

(*e*)   _____   1

(*f*)   _____   1

[Turn over for Question 7 on *Page eight*

7.   **"Conventions are alternative ways of presenting parts of a drama."**

Marks

Describe how conventions were effectively used during your Standard Grade course. You must refer to **three** different conventions. (These need not all come from the same drama.)

Convention 1 _____

_____

_____

_____

_____

4

Convention 2 _____

_____

_____

_____

_____

4

Convention 3 _____

_____

_____

_____

_____

4

[END OF QUESTION PAPER]

STANDARD GRADE | FOUNDATION | GENERAL | CREDIT

2008

[BLANK PAGE]

FGC

0700/404

NATIONAL QUALIFICATIONS 2008	TUESDAY, 20 MAY F: 9.00 AM – 9.45 AM G: 10.05 AM – 10.50 AM C: 11.10 AM – 12.10 PM	DRAMA STANDARD GRADE Foundation, General and Credit Levels Stimulus Paper

Study carefully the five stimuli (i), (ii), (iii), (iv) and (v) before answering the questions in Section A of the Question Paper.

STIMULUS (i)

"Silver dance shoes in her pocket,
No one's photo in her locket"

The Lady of Shallot **by Liz Lochhead**

STIMULUS (ii)

STIMULUS (iii)

And so even though we face the difficulties of today and tomorrow, I still have a dream. It is a dream deeply rooted in the American dream.

I have a dream that one day this nation will rise up and live out the true meaning of its creed: "We hold these truths to be self-evident, that all men are created equal."

Martin Luther King Jr., Speech at Civil Rights March on Washington, August 28, 1963

STIMULUS (iv)

Urgent!   Phone home asap.

[Turn over for Stimulus (v) on *Page four*

STIMULUS (v)

MAGGIE:	Whit kind o talk is this, Jenny? Did ye no think o us. Yer daddy an me?
JENNY:	Think o ye? Oh aye, Mammy, I thought o ye. But thinking jist made me greet. I was that ashamed o masel . . . Isa and me, we were that rotten tae ye, the things we said.
MAGGIE:	That's a bye, Jenny.
JENNY:	Naethin's ever *bye,* Mammy; it's a there, like a photy-album in yer heid . . . I kept seein ma daddy, the way he used tae sing tae me when I wis wee; I seen him holdin ma bare feet in his hands tae warm them an feedin me bread an hot milk oot o a blue cup. (*Pause*) I don't know where you were, Mammy.
LILY:	Ben the back room wi the midwife, likely. (*Pause*) It's as weel ye came tae yer senses; yon's no the way tae tak oot o yer troubles; a river. But ye're daein fine noo? Ye merriet?
JENNY:	No.

Act III *Men Should Weep* by Ena Lamont Stewart

[END OF STIMULUS PAPER]

FOR OFFICIAL USE

F

Total

0700/401

NATIONAL
QUALIFICATIONS
2008

TUESDAY, 20 MAY
9.00 AM – 9.45 AM

DRAMA
STANDARD GRADE
Foundation Level

Fill in these boxes and read what is printed below.

Full name of centre

Town

Forename(s)

Surname

Date of birth

Day Month Year   Scottish candidate number   Number of seat

1 Read each question carefully.

2 Attempt **all** questions in **both** sections.

3 You may use sketches and diagrams to illustrate your answers.

4 All answers are to be written in this answer book. If there is not enough space for you to complete your answer to any question, **additional paper** can be obtained from the invigilator.

5 The Stimuli for Section A are supplied in a separate paper. Check that you have this paper before the examination begins.

6 Before leaving the examination room you must give this book to the invigilator. If you do not, you may lose all the marks for this paper.

SECTION A

Answer **all** of the following questions.

> Your answers should be based
> on work from the **stimulus material**.
> (*A copy of the Stimulus Paper is provided.*)

My group chose stimulus _____ (*enter number from Stimulus Paper*).

1.   How many scenes were in your drama?

    _____

    1

2.   (*a*)   Describe what happened in **one** scene that you were in.

    _____

    _____

    _____

    _____

    _____

    3

    (*b*)   What music **or** sound effect would you like to have used in this scene?
    Say why.

    _____

    _____

    _____

    2

Marks

3.   Complete the following information for **your character.**

Full name: _____ Age: _____   1

Occupation: _____   1

Appearance: _____

_____

_____

_____   3

Describe the costume worn by your character.

_____

_____

_____

_____   3

[Turn over

DO NOT
WRITE IN
THIS MARGIN

Marks

4. (*a*) What was the **most important moment** in your drama for **your character**?

_____

_____   1

(*b*) Why was that moment important?

_____

_____   1

(*c*) How did your character **speak** and/or **move** at that moment?

_____

_____

_____

_____

_____

_____

_____

_____   4

Marks

5. In the space below draw a ground plan of the acting area for **one** scene of your drama.

This scene takes place in _____

Key:

5

Marks

SECTION B

Answer **all** of the following questions.

Your answers should **not** be based
on work from the **stimulus material**.

6. Look at the words below and write **seven** of them in the appropriate columns.

Fade in	Exit	Jewellery	Flood	Fade down
Thrust	Hats	Gel	Blackout	Scene

Lighting	Sound	Costume

7

[Turn over for Question 7 on *Page eight*

Marks

7. Look carefully at the characters pictured below.

Now read questions (*a*) to (*h*) before writing your answers.

Character A   Character B

(*a*) Who do you think these two characters are?

Character A _____   **1**

Character B _____   **1**

Imagine that these two characters are entering a lift in a large office building.

(*b*) Choose either character A **or** B. Describe their movement.

_____

_____

_____   **2**

DO NOT
WRITE IN
THIS MARGIN

Marks

7.   (continued)

Imagine one character speaks to the other.

(*c*) What might they say?

_____   1

(*d*) How might they say it?

_____   1

The lift suddenly stops between floors.

(*e*) Choose either character A **or** B. Describe their movement.

_____

_____

_____   2

Imagine one character speaks to the other now.

(*f*) What might they say now?

_____   1

(*g*) How might they say it?

_____   1

(*h*) What do you think will happen next to these two characters?

_____

_____

_____   2

[Turn over

8. Read the following questions and put a tick (✓) in the box next to the correct answer.

Marks

(*a*) Loudness or quietness of the voice

☐ dialogue
☐ monologue
☐ volume
☐ clarity

(*b*) A movement of the hand or arm which communicates a meaning or emotion

☐ body language
☐ gesture
☐ cue
☐ pace

(*c*) The speed of speech or movement

☐ pace
☐ accent
☐ intonation
☐ practice

(*d*) A look on a face which shows emotion

☐ scenario
☐ smile
☐ eye contact
☐ facial expression

(*e*) Way of speaking used in a local area or country

☐ tone
☐ accent
☐ tension
☐ fluency

(*f*) Messages given by the position or movement of body

☐ convention
☐ mime
☐ body language
☐ gesture

6

[END OF QUESTION PAPER]

FOR OFFICIAL USE

G

Total

0700/402

NATIONAL
QUALIFICATIONS
2008

TUESDAY, 20 MAY
10.05 AM – 10.50 AM

DRAMA
STANDARD GRADE
General Level

FILL In these boxes and read what is printed below.

Full name of centre

Town

Forename(s)

Surname

Date of birth
Day Month Year   Scottish candidate number   Number of seat

1 Read each question carefully.

2 Attempt **all** questions in **both** sections.

3 You may use sketches and diagrams to illustrate your answers.

4 All answers are to be written in this answer book. If there is not enough space for you to complete your answer to any question, **additional paper** can be obtained from the invigilator.

5 The Stimuli for Section A are supplied in a separate paper. Check that you have this paper before the examination begins.

6 Before leaving the examination room you must give this book to the invigilator. If you do not, you may lose all the marks for this paper.

[BLANK PAGE]

DO NOT
WRITE IN
THIS MARGIN

Marks

SECTION A

Answer **all** of the following questions.

> Your answers should be based
> on work from the **stimulus material**.
> (*A copy of the Stimulus Paper is provided.*)

My group chose stimulus _____ (*enter number from stimulus paper*).

1. Use the space below to write a **brief scenario** of the drama created by your group.

Scene number	Time, place and action

6

Marks

2. Think about the most important relationship between **your character** and **one other character**.

   (*a*) What was the relationship between these two characters?

_____

_____

_____   2

   (*b*) Complete the following character information for **that other** character.

Name of character: _____ Age: _____   1

Occupation: _____   1

Physical Description: _____

_____

_____   2

Personality: _____

_____

_____   2

   (*c*) What was the **most important moment** in your drama for the relationship between these two characters? Why?

_____

_____

_____

_____

_____   3

Marks

2. **(continued)**

   (*d*)   How did you and the other actor use voice and movement to highlight the importance of **that moment**?

_____

_____

_____

_____

_____

_____

_____

_____

_____

6

[Turn over

Marks

3. Look at the following **theatre arts** terms. Select **four** of these and say when you could have used them in your group's drama.

follow spot	live (SFX)	cross fade
rostra	stage make up	personal prop

(a) _____ could have been used when _____

_____ 1

(b) _____ could have been used when _____

_____ 1

(c) _____ could have been used when _____

_____ 1

(d) _____ could have been used when _____

_____ 1

4. What would have been the ideal venue and target audience for your drama? Say why.

_____

_____

_____

_____

_____ 3

SECTION B

Marks

Answer **all** of the following questions.

> Your answers should **not** be based on work from the
> **stimulus material**.

5. Complete the following definitions.

(*a*) Stage within an enclosing arch.

_____ 　1

(*b*) Change of voice to express emotion.

_____ 　1

(*c*) Recall of words said about a character or situation.

_____ 　1

(*d*) A conversation between two or more characters.

_____ 　1

(*e*) Questioning a character in role.

_____ 　1

(*f*) Drama created 'on the spot' without a script or plan.

_____ 　1

[Turn over

Marks

6.   *A ground plan is a bird's eye view of the set.*

A fully correct ground plan must include certain details. List **five** of these.

(i) _____   1

(ii) _____   1

(iii) _____   1

(iv) _____   1

(v) _____   1

7.   *The purpose of a drama must be established in order to
communicate meaning.*

List **three** examples of purpose.

(i) _____   1

(ii) _____   1

(iii) _____   1

DO NOT
WRITE IN
THIS MARGIN

Marks

Read the following question carefully before answering parts (*a*) and (*b*).

8. Imagine that you have been asked to devise a **movement piece** in two scenes under the following titles.

Scene 1   Lost in the City

Scene 2   Found

(*a*) Describe in detail the **movement** in each of these two scenes.

Scene 1 _____

_____

_____

_____

_____

_____

_____

_____

_____

4

Scene 2 _____

_____

_____

_____

_____

_____

_____

_____

_____

4

[Turn over

Marks

8.   (continued)

(*b*)   How would you use **theatre arts** to enhance this movement piece? Indicate which theatre arts you would use, when you would use them and why. Refer to **at least two** theatre arts in your answer.

8

[END OF QUESTION PAPER]

FOR OFFICIAL USE

C

Total

0700/403

NATIONAL
QUALIFICATIONS
2008

TUESDAY, 20 MAY
11.10 AM – 12.10 PM

DRAMA
STANDARD GRADE
Credit Level

Fill in these boxes and read what is printed below.

Full name of centre

Town

Forename(s)

Surname

Date of birth

Day Month Year   Scottish candidate number   Number of seat

1 Read each question carefully.

2 Attempt **all** questions in **both** sections.

3 You may use sketches and diagrams to illustrate your answers.

4 All answers are to be written in this answer book. If there is not enough space for you to complete your answer to any question, **additional paper** can be obtained from the invigilator.

5 The Stimuli for Section A are supplied in a separate paper. Check that you have this paper before the examination begins.

6 Before leaving the examination room you must give this book to the invigilator. If you do not, you may lose all the marks for this paper.

Marks

SECTION A

Answer **all** of the following questions.

Your answers should be based
on work from the **stimulus material**.
(*A copy of the Stimulus Paper is provided.*)

My group chose stimulus _____ (*enter number from Stimulus Paper*).

1. (*a*) Identify the main strength of your final presentation.

    _____   1

    (*b*) Which aspect of the drama process contributed most to this?

    _____

    _____   1

    (*c*) Give reasons for your answer.

    _____

    _____

    _____   2

2. (*a*) Identify the main weakness of your final presentation.

    _____   1

    (*b*) Which aspect of the drama process contributed most to this?

    _____

    _____   1

    (*c*) Give reasons for your answer.

    _____

    _____

    _____   2

DO NOT
WRITE IN
THIS MARGIN

Marks

3. (*a*) Name **two** characters of differing status in your drama.

Character 1 _____

Character 2 _____

(*b*) Describe the status of each character.

Character 1 _____

_____

_____

_____

2

Character 2 _____

_____

_____

_____

2

(*c*) How was this difference in status shown in performance?

_____

_____

_____

_____

_____

_____

_____

_____

4

(*d*) Write 'in role' how the character **played by you** felt about one of those characters.

_____

_____

_____

_____

_____

_____

_____

4

DO NOT
WRITE IN
THIS MARGI

Marks

SECTION B

Answer **all** of the following questions.

> Your answers should **not** be based
> on work from the **stimulus material**.

4. Read the following and then answer the questions.

David is fun-loving and outrageous! He is sixteen and a "party animal". He has lots of friends.

Vicky wants to go into politics. She is seventeen and enjoys reading. She has a few friends — most are older than her.

Imagine that you are to design David and Vicky's "look". Describe their costume and general appearance.

(a) David _____

_____

_____

_____

_____

_____   6

(b) Vicky _____

_____

_____

_____

_____

_____   6

5. Think back to a character that you successfully portrayed in your Standard Grade Drama course.

Marks

(*a*) Describe that character.

_____

_____

_____

_____

_____   **3**

(*b*) List **five** characterisation techniques you used, or could have used, to develop this character.

1 _____

2 _____

3 _____

4 _____

5 _____   **5**

(*c*) Choose **one** from the list above and say how this technique helped you, or might have helped you, to develop a greater understanding of this character.

_____

_____

_____

_____

_____

_____   **4**

[Turn over

Marks

6. Write the correct word after each definition.

(*a*) Person who has written the play _____   1

(*b*) Sides of a theatre stage _____   1

(*c*) Actions or remarks whose significance is not realised by all the characters

_____   1

(*d*) Rising and falling of voice in speech _____   1

(*e*) Piece of scenery on wheels for ease of movement _____   1

(*f*) Slope of stage (to allow actors to be seen) _____   1

(*g*) Thin metal plate cut out in a pattern and placed in a lantern to project pattern or shape into the acting area

_____   1

(*h*) Stage fireworks _____   1

7. The following excerpt is from the opening scene of *Iron* by *Rona Munro*. Read it carefully and then answer the questions.

Act One

The sounds of a woman's prison just before lockdown.

GUARD 1 (*roars from offstage*). Lock down! Lock down!

Waiting room. A small area outside the visitor's room. This is where visitors wait for their names to be called. Josie is sitting here, alone. She seems unperturbed, pleasantly interested in her surroundings. Her clothes are fashionable but very low key. She wears black. She looks very plain and very expensive. She's just waiting, perfectly composed.

After a moment GUARD 2 *enters, she looks at* JOSIE *for a moment without saying anything.* JOSIE *looks back, she smiles pleasantly.*

GUARD 2. You're here to see Prisoner Black?

JOSIE. That's right.

GUARD 2 (*shaking head*). Never thought I'd see the day . . .

JOSIE. Is there a problem? You didn't call my name.

GUARD 2. So who are you?

JOSIE. Josie . . . Josie Kerr? I'm . . . She was my mother.

Pause. GUARD 2 *is completely flabbergasted.*

GUARD 2. You're her daughter?

[Turn over

Marks

7. **(continued)**

(*a*) Now focus on the **waiting room** mentioned in the script extract.

Describe the appearance of the set. You should demonstrate how the set itself, the set dressings, colours and set props reflect the room's mood and atmosphere.

The mood and atmosphere I would create in this room is _____

_____

This is how I would create it _____

_____

_____

_____

_____

_____

_____

_____

_____

_____

_____

_____

_____

_____

8

Marks

7. (continued)

Look again at the dialogue between the two characters printed below and imagine that you are going to direct this scene.

> GUARD 2. You're here to see Prisoner Black?
>
> JOSIE. That's right.
>
> GUARD 2 (*shaking head*). Never thought I'd see the day . . .
>
> JOSIE. Is there a problem? You didn't call my name.
>
> GUARD 2. So who are you?
>
> JOSIE. Josie . . . Josie Kerr? I'm . . . She was my mother.
>
> *Pause.* GUARD 2 *is completely flabbergasted*.
>
> GUARD 2. You're her daughter?

(b) Make notes for the actors to assist them in their portrayal of these characters.

GUARD 2 _____

_____

_____

_____

_____

_____

_____

5

JOSIE _____

_____

_____

_____

_____

_____

_____

5

[END OF QUESTION PAPER]

[BLANK PAGE]

2009

[BLANK PAGE]

F
G
C

0700/404

NATIONAL
QUALIFICATIONS
2009

THURSDAY, 21 MAY
F: 9.00 AM – 9.45 AM
G: 10.05 AM – 10.50 AM
C: 11.10 AM – 12.10 PM

DRAMA
STANDARD GRADE
Foundation, General
and Credit Levels
Stimulus Paper

Study carefully the five stimuli (i), (ii), (iii), (iv) and (v)
before answering the questions in Section A of the
Question Paper.

STIMULUS (i)

Then let us pray that come it may,
As come it will for a' that;
That sense and worth, o'er a' the earth,
May bear the gree, and a' that.
For a' that and a' that,
It's coming yet for a' that,
That man to man, the world o'er,
Shall brothers be for a' that.

For A' That and A' That
Robert Burns 1795

STIMULUS (ii)

STIMULUS (iii)

"Fools rush in where angels fear to tread"

STIMULUS (iv)

Hush, little baby, don't say a word,
Mama's gonna buy you a mockingbird.

And if that mockingbird won't sing,
Mama's gonna buy you a diamond ring.

And if that diamond ring turns brass,
Mama's gonna buy you a looking glass.

And if that looking glass gets broke,
Mama's gonna buy you a billy goat.

And if that billy goat won't pull,
Mama's gonna buy you a cart and bull.

And if that cart and bull turn over,
Mama's gonna buy you a dog named Rover.

And if that dog named Rover won't bark,
Mama's gonna buy you a horse and cart.

And if that horse and cart fall down,
You'll still be the sweetest little baby in town.

Anon.

[Turn over for Stimulus (v) on *Page four*

STIMULUS (v)

[END OF STIMULUS PAPER]

FOR OFFICIAL USE

F

Total

0700/401

NATIONAL
QUALIFICATIONS
2009

THURSDAY, 21 MAY
9.00 AM – 9.45 AM

DRAMA
STANDARD GRADE
Foundation Level

Fill in these boxes and read what is printed below.

Full name of centre

Town

Forename(s)

Surname

Date of birth

Day Month Year   Scottish candidate number   Number of seat

1 Read each question carefully.

2 Attempt **all** questions in **both** sections.

3 You may use sketches and diagrams to illustrate your answers.

4 All answers are to be written in this answer book. If there is not enough space for you to complete your answer to any question, **additional paper** can be obtained from the invigilator.

5 The Stimuli for Section A are supplied in a separate paper. Check that you have this paper before the examination begins.

6 Before leaving the examination room you must give this book to the invigilator. If you do not, you may lose all the marks for this paper.

SECTION A

Marks

Answer **all** of the following questions.

> Your answers should be based
> on work from the **stimulus material**.
> (*A copy of the Stimulus Paper is provided.*)

My group chose stimulus _____ (*enter number from Stimulus Paper*).

1.   Describe the action during the **last scene** of your group's drama.

   _____

   _____

   _____

   _____

   _____

   _____   3

2.   In the space below draw the ground plan for that **last scene**.

   Key:

5

DO NOT
WRITE IN
THIS MARGIN

Marks

3. Theatre arts include **lighting**, **sound and props**.

In what ways would you use **two** of these in your **last scene**?

Theatre art number 1 _____

_____

_____

_____

2

Theatre art number 2 _____

_____

_____

_____

2

4. Complete the following information for **your character**.

Full name: _____ Age: _____   1

Occupation: _____   1

Appearance: _____

_____

_____

2

[Turn over

Marks

5. Read all of the parts of this question before you start to answer.

Now, think about all the scenes in the drama created by your group.

(*a*) What part of the action do you think was the most exciting?

_____

_____   1

(*b*) Give a reason for your answer.

_____   1

(*c*) Name **one** character in that part of the action.

_____   1

(*d*) How did that character **speak** at that exciting part of the action?

_____

_____

_____   2

(*e*) How did that character **move** at that exciting part of the action?

_____

_____

_____   2

6. When your group were developing your drama from **stimulus** to **presentation**, which part of the process did you find most difficult? Say why.

_____

_____

_____

_____   2

DO NOT
WRITE IN
THIS MARGIN

Marks

SECTION B

Answer **all** of the following questions.

Your answers should **not** be based
on work from the **stimulus material**.
---

7. Look at these two faces and read the character information written below each
   picture.

Character A   Character B

Name: John Robertson   Name: Judith Evans
Age: 65   Age: 27
Occupation: Retired gardener   Occupation: Doctor

List two **personal props** and two items of **costume** for these characters.

Character A   **Character B**

Personal prop 1 _____   Personal prop 1 _____   2

Personal prop 2 _____   Personal prop 2 _____   2

Costume 1 _____   Costume 1 _____   2

Costume 2 _____   Costume 2 _____   2

[Turn over

Marks

8. Read the following information then answer the questions below.

> *Sharon has entered a talent competition*
> *She has just finished her performance and is waiting for the result.*

(a) Describe Sharon's movement at this time.

_____

_____   2

(b) What might she say?

_____   1

(c) How might she say it?

_____

_____   2

Now, you decide whether she wins or loses.

Tick the box.   Win ☐ **or   Lose** ☐

(d) Describe Sharon's movement after she hears the result.

_____

_____   2

(e) What might she say now?

_____   1

(f) How might she say it?

_____

_____   2

DO NOT
WRITE IN
THIS MARGIN

Marks

9. Read the definitions below and write the correct word in the space provided.

(*a*) The practice or preparation of a drama is called a

_____   1

(*b*) When a character speaks their thoughts aloud it is called a

_____   1

(*c*) A lantern giving a wide spread of light is a

_____   1

(*d*) Blocks or platforms used to create levels are

_____   1

(*e*) To come on stage is to

_____   1

(*f*) The build up of excitement in a drama is called

_____   1

(*g*) The speed of speech or movement is called

_____   1

[*END OF QUESTION PAPER*]

[BLANK PAGE]

FOR OFFICIAL USE

G

Total

0700/402

NATIONAL
QUALIFICATIONS
2009

THURSDAY, 21 MAY
10.05 AM – 10.50 AM

DRAMA
STANDARD GRADE
General Level

Fill in these boxes and read what is printed below.

Full name of centre

Town

Forename(s)

Surname

Date of birth

Day Month Year   Scottish candidate number   Number of seat

1 Read each question carefully.

2 Attempt **all** questions in **both** sections.

3 You may use sketches and diagrams to illustrate your answers.

4 All answers are to be written in this answer book. If there is not enough space for you to complete your answer to any question, **additional paper** can be obtained from the invigilator.

5 The Stimuli for Section A are supplied in a separate paper. Check that you have this paper before the examination begins.

6 Before leaving the examination room you must give this book to the invigilator. If you do not, you may lose all the marks for this paper.

Marks

SECTION A

Answer **all** of the following questions.

> Your answers should be based
> on work from the **stimulus material**.
> (*A copy of the Stimulus Paper is provided.*)

My group chose stimulus _____ (*enter number from stimulus paper*).

1. Use the space below to write a **brief scenario** of the drama created by your group.

Scene number	Time, place and action

6

Marks

2. (*a*) If you could change one aspect of your drama what would it be?

_____

_____   1

(*b*) Give **two** reasons for your answer.

_____

_____

_____

_____   2

3. (*a*) Name **two** important characters in your drama. What roles did they play?

Character 1 _____

Role _____   1

Character 2 _____

Role _____   1

(*b*) How would an audience have felt towards these two characters? Give reasons
for your answer.

Character 1 _____

_____

_____   2

Character 2 _____

_____

_____   2

[Turn over

Marks

4. Read all parts of the question before answering.

(*a*) Give the following details for the character played by you.

Full name and age _____   **1**

List **three** aspects of your character's personality.

1 _____

_____   **1**

2 _____

_____   **1**

3 _____

_____   **1**

(*b*) In what ways would you use costume, make-up and personal props to help portray your character's personality?

Give reasons for your answer.

_____

_____

_____

_____

_____

_____

_____

_____

_____

_____

_____

_____   **7**

DO NOT
WRITE IN
THIS MARGIN

Marks

4. (continued)

(*c*) How do you think your character would behave when meeting new people for the first time?

Voice

_____

_____

_____

_____

2

Movement

_____

_____

_____

_____

2

[Turn over

DO NOT
WRITE IN
THIS MARGIN

Marks

SECTION B

Answer **all** of the following questions.

> Your answers should **not** be based on work from the
> **stimulus material**.

5. Write the correct word(s) in the space provided.

    (*a*) A character's importance relative to others.

    _____   1

    (*b*) The whole acting area is evenly lit.

    _____   1

    (*c*) Storyline of the drama.

    _____   1

    (*d*) Lantern giving a soft edged beam of light.

    _____   1

6. Read the following short script carefully then answer the questions below.

Mr Andrews:	And who does this belong to, then?
Sam:	Oh no. He's found it!
Alex:	Stay calm.
Dee:	Why is this happening to me?

(*a*) Describe, **using voice terms**, how each character would speak their line. (It is possible to use the same voice term more than once.)

Mr Andrews: And who does this belong to, then?

_____

_____   2

Sam: Oh no. He's found it!

_____

_____   2

Alex: Stay calm.

_____

_____   2

Dee: Why is this happening to me?

_____

_____   2

[Turn over

6.   **(continued)**

(*b*)   Describe, **using movement terms**, how each character would move when saying each line.

(It is possible to use the same movement term more than once.)

Mr Andrews: And who does this belong to, then?

_____

_____   2

Sam: Oh no. He's found it!

_____

_____   2

Alex: Stay calm.

_____

_____   2

Dee: Why is this happening to me?

_____

_____   2

Marks

7. Look at the following theatre posters.

On the line below each poster, write which **drama form** is being used.

(a)

> ### Cinderella
>
> "The best entertainment this Christmas"

_____

(b)

> ### The Wizard of Oz
>
> "The famous play with the famous songs"

_____

(c)

> ### My Life
>
> "A solo performance of outstanding quality"

_____

(d)

> ### Street Life
>
> "An emotional tale told through dance"

_____

(e)

> ### Stop Me Please!
>
> "The funniest drama of the season"

_____

(f)

> ### Men Should Weep
>
> "Don't miss this drama"

_____

6

[Turn over

8. Match each of the following drama terms to its correct definition. Do this by drawing an arrow each time, as in the example below.

Marks

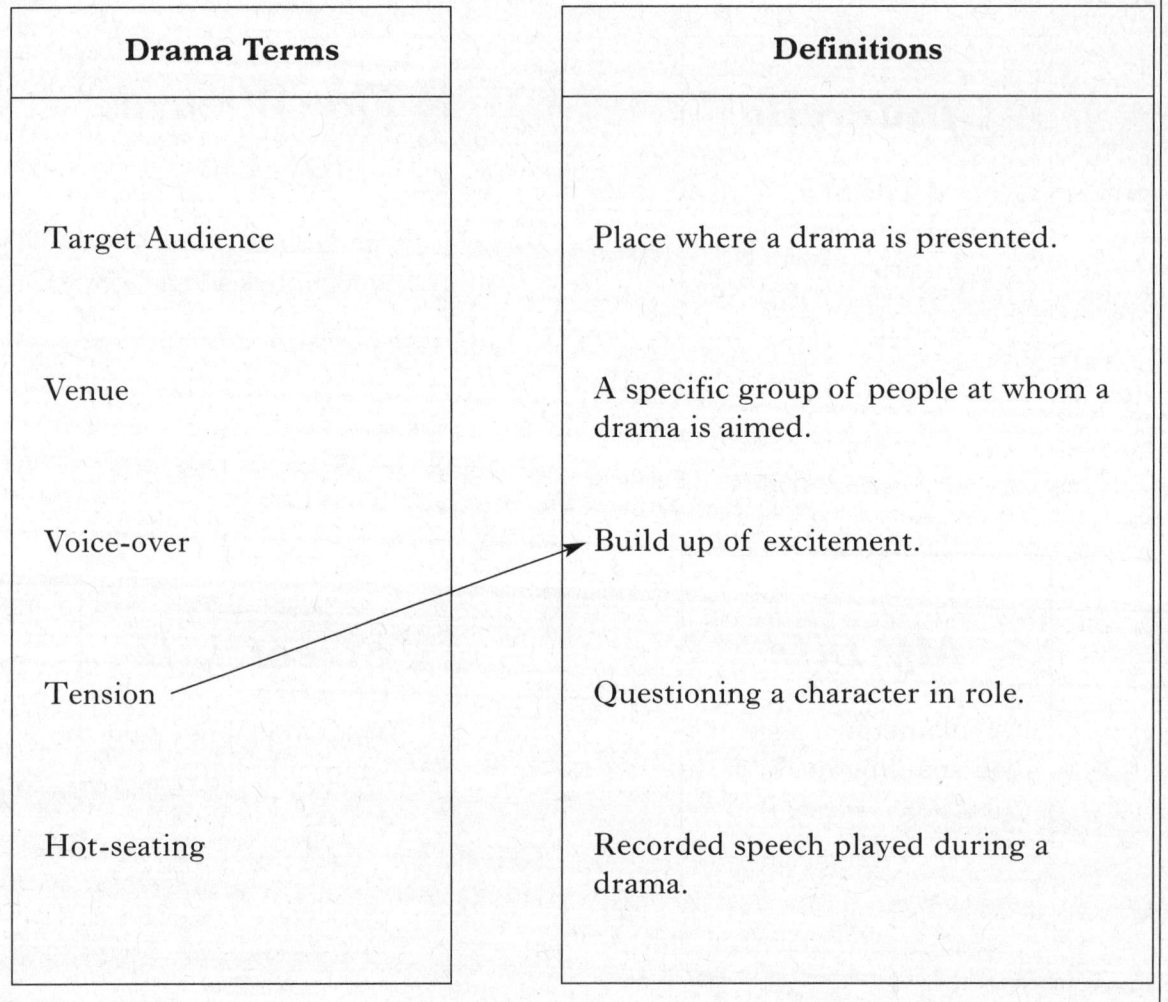

Drama Terms	Definitions
Target Audience	Place where a drama is presented.
Venue	A specific group of people at whom a drama is aimed.
Voice-over	Build up of excitement.
Tension	Questioning a character in role.
Hot-seating	Recorded speech played during a drama.

4

[END OF QUESTION PAPER]

FOR OFFICIAL USE

C

Total

0700/403

NATIONAL
QUALIFICATIONS
2009

THURSDAY, 21 MAY
11.10 AM – 12.10 PM

DRAMA
STANDARD GRADE
Credit Level

Fill in these boxes and read what is printed below.

Full name of centre

Town

Forename(s)

Surname

Date of birth

Day Month Year

Scottish candidate number

Number of seat

1 Read each question carefully.

2 Attempt **all** questions in **both** sections.

3 You may use sketches and diagrams to illustrate your answers.

4 All answers are to be written in this answer book. If there is not enough space for you to complete your answer to any question, **additional paper** can be obtained from the invigilator.

5 The Stimuli for Section A are supplied in a separate paper. Check that you have this paper before the examination begins.

6 Before leaving the examination room you must give this book to the invigilator. If you do not, you may lose all the marks for this paper.

[BLANK PAGE]

DO NOT
WRITE IN
THIS MARGIN

Marks

SECTION A

Answer **all** of the following questions.

> Your answers should be based
> on work from the **stimulus material**.
> (*A copy of the Stimulus Paper is provided.*)

My group chose stimulus _____ (*enter number from Stimulus Paper*).

1.
> **Structure is the way in which time, place and action are sequenced.**
> Structure can be linear or non-linear.

How did the structure of your drama help to make it more effective?

_____

_____

_____

_____

_____

3

[Turn over

Marks

2. (*a*) Identify and justify what you consider to be the climax of your drama.

_____

_____

_____

_____

_____

_____

3

(*b*) In what way could you use the acting techniques of **eye-contact**, **contrast and timing** to highlight this climax?

_____

_____

_____

_____

_____

_____

_____

_____

_____

_____

6

Marks

3.   Imagine your drama is to be performed to an audience.

Make notes, using the bullet points below, to indicate your requirements for:

      lighting
      sound
      set
      set dressings.

- _____

   _____

- _____

   _____

- _____

   _____

- _____

   _____

- _____

   _____

- _____

   _____

- _____

   _____

   _____

8

[Turn over

Marks

SECTION B

Answer **all** of the following questions.

Your answers should **not** be based
on work from the **stimulus material**.

4. Look carefully at this plan, which is a bird's eye view of a theatre. Now, answer the
    questions on the opposite page.

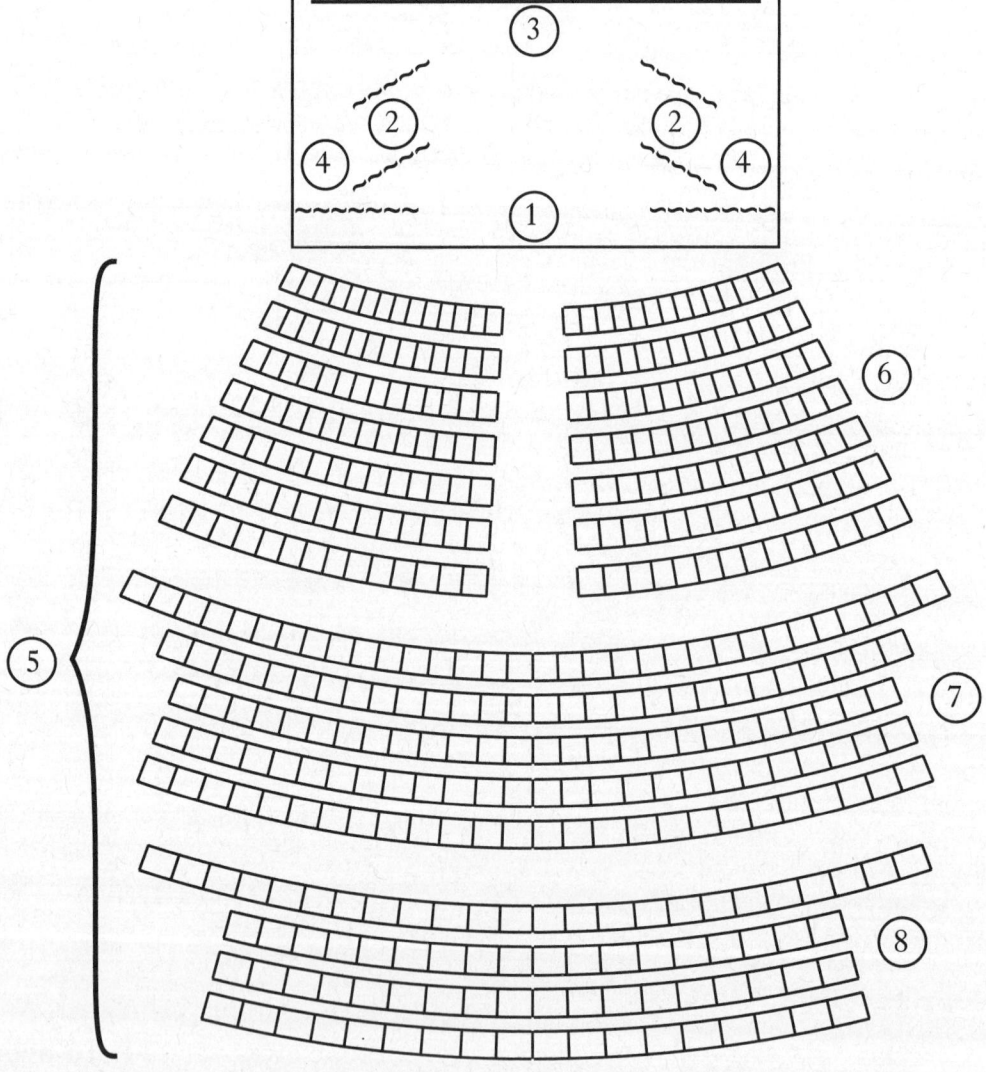

Marks

4. (continued)

(*a*) What is the name of this part of the stage ☐1 which is in front of the curtain?

_____

1

(*b*) These drapes ☐2 close off the sides, or back, of the stage. What are they called?

_____

1

(*c*) What is the name given to ☐3 , the back wall of the stage?

_____

1

(*d*) What are the sides of the theatre stage ☐4 called?

_____

1

(*e*) What is the name given to this whole part of the theatre, ☐5 , which is for the audience and filled with seats?

_____

1

(*f*) What are the three levels of seating ☐6 , ☐7 and ☐8 called?

☐6 _____

1

☐7 _____

1

☐8 _____

1

[Turn over

Marks

5. The following is a script extract from a drama presentation. Read it carefully before answering the questions.

Sir George:	Why Miranda, what has come over you?
Miranda:	I simply can't go on like this any longer!
Sir George:	I'm sure you'll calm down after the wedding. Isn't that right Henry?
Henry:	Of course Sir George! She's naturally just excited about marrying me.
Miranda:	Aaagh! . . . I've had enough. Henry, I WILL NEVER MARRY YOU!
Henry: **Sir George**:	} WHAT!?

Describe how facial expression, body language and gesture could be used when playing these characters.

Sir George's facial expression, body language and gesture:

_____

_____

_____

_____

_____

_____

3

DO NOT
WRITE IN
THIS MARGIN

Marks

5. (continued)

Miranda's facial expression, body language and gesture:

_____

_____

_____

_____

_____

3

Henry's facial expression, body language and gesture:

_____

_____

_____

_____

_____

3

[Turn over

Marks

6. Read all of the following information, and questions (*a*) to (*c*), before answering.

The Enchanted Forest

Lights fade up.
Enter two characters, The Woman and The Boy.
They are dressed unusually.
The Boy starts to search the forest floor. The Woman assists,
but looks off-stage as if expecting someone or something.

(*a*) As a director, how would you heighten the **tension** in this extract? Refer to movement and motivation.

_____

_____

_____

_____

_____

_____

_____

_____

_____

_____

_____

_____

_____

8

DO NOT
WRITE IN
THIS MARGIN

Marks

6. **(continued)**

(b) Describe each character's "unusual" costume.

The Woman _____

_____

_____

_____

_____

4

The Boy _____

_____

_____

_____

_____

4

(c) Describe your stage make-up concepts for either The Woman or The Boy.

_____

_____

_____

_____

_____

4

(d) Imagine that you are to use one special effect. What would it be, in what ways would you use it and what effect do you hope it would have?

_____

_____

_____

_____

_____

_____

5

Marks

7. Think of a time during your Standard Grade Drama course when you participated in a particularly effective drama.

What, in your opinion, made the drama successful?

_____

_____

_____

_____

_____

_____

_____

_____

_____

_____

_____

_____

_____

_____

8

[END OF QUESTION PAPER]

STANDARD GRADE | FOUNDATION | GENERAL | CREDIT

2010

[BLANK PAGE]

SQA STANDARD GRADE
FOUNDATION, GENERAL AND CREDIT
DRAMA 2006–2010

DRAMA FOUNDATION
2006

SECTION A

1. Although scene, time and place are not asked for, the word scenario implies a scene by scene account. Beginning/middle/end should be fully and well summarised.

2. **Name.** Full name (not own) and age required for mark
   Occupation. "None" will not be accepted
   Personality. Each aspect given will gain one mark
   Appearance. Each aspect given will gain one mark. May be physical appearance/style of dress, distinguishing marks etc.
   Information. Must be relevant to character/scenario

3. (a) Moment must be identified or implicit, if not mentioned, in scenario.
      Moment must be small part of scene ie, not "Scene 1" or "the end".

   (b) Justifications may include character/plot development, climax, impact on audience, mood/atmosphere/tension

   (c) One mark for each point made

   (d) One mark for each point made

   (e) Must be consistent with identified moment and contain some detail

4. One mark each for:
   - set (overhead view, ie no legs on table/chairs)
   - audience
   - entrance/exits
   - key
   - practicality/scale and delineation of acting area

SECTION B

5. (a) dance drama

   (b) pace

   (c) dress rehearsal

   (d) scenario

   (e) tension

   (f) cue

   (g) gesture

6. (a)/(b) Full name, role or both
   (c) More than a brief description needed for two marks. Must refer to both characters.

   (d) 'When' and 'where' required. For 'when' a broad statement about 'present day' or specifies "Saturday, 4 o'clock" is acceptable.

(e) Must be lead-up to (c). One mark for generalised statement like "He was in trouble at school", two for a more detailed statement.

(f)/(g) Single word answer sufficient

(h) Both characters must be mentioned in the answer. Wholly appropriate and/or imaginative development given the information contained in (a)-(g) should be shown.

7. **Drama Forms** – musical, pantomime, play
   Drama Conventions – flashback, freeze frame, slow motion

DRAMA GENERAL 2006

SECTION A

1. Answers should be brief. Over-long scenarios will be penalised. ("Over-long" means excessive detail, not excessive number of scenes)
    Scenario
    Progression is clear and plot succinctly summarised
    Time/Place
    All changes in time and place given

2. (*a*) Provide the correct name of three characters and the role of each.
    (*b*) One mark for simple statement, two for fuller answer/justification
    (*c*) Reference required to both voice **and** movement. Must be consistent with relationship outlined in (*b*).

3. **Name/Age**. Full name **and** age are required for mark
    Occupation. "None" will not be accepted
    Physical description. Two points required for two marks
    Personality. Two points required for two marks
    Costume. One mark awarded for each item of costume. Three marks possible for two items if fully described. Must be consistent with character/scenario.
    Personal props. One mark awarded for each personal prop. Three marks possible for two items if fully described. Must be consistent with character/ scenario

4. One mark per challenge, one mark per solution.

SECTION B

5. Voice **and** movement must be referred to in Sc.1 and/or Sc.2
    Ideas in Sc.2 may be new or changes to those in Sc.1.
    Voice and movement must relate to information given about Danny.

6. *"Mime is a stylised form of movement which creates an illusion of reality."*
    (BofK P.14) or something *very* close is required for two marks. One mark will be awarded for other valid definitions which show understanding of the term.
    S. Simple, P. Precise, E. Exaggerated, C. Clear, S. Slow
    "Slow and Simple in any order."
    No alternatives. One mark for each.

7. Left/Right, Up/Down and Centre correctly labelled

8. **Set/Set dressing**
    A response showing clear understanding of how set/set dressings can accompany the scene
    Lighting
    A response and range of ideas showing clear understanding of how lighting can accompany the scene
    Sound
    A response and range of ideas showing clear understanding of how sound can accompany the scene

DRAMA CREDIT
2006

SECTION A

1. (*a*) **Source: BofK P.17**
   A drama can be used for the following purposes, singly or in combination, to:
   - communicate a message
   - entertain
   - tell a story
   - educate
   - explore a theme/issue
   - explore and experience.
     (eg through audience participation, forum/theatre)
   - Paraphrases of these or any other valid answer
   (*b*) Ways of knowing may include:
   - feedback from teacher, cast, peers, audience
   - audience reaction
   - empirical evidence
   - video review
   Positive or negative response acceptable. One mark each for any two of the above, or other, valid answers.

2. (*a*) Part clearly identified for one mark. Wide definition of 'part' is acceptable.
   (*b*) Answers may include reference to performance skills, theatre arts, conventions, mood/atmosphere/tension, message, form, organisation.
   Must relate to (*a*). One mark for each valid point made.

3. (*a*) One mark for identification of character. Full name not required here.
   (*b*) *May include reference to such aspects as voice, movement, characterisation, relationship with other characters, actor/audience relationship, timing, use of costume/props etc.*
   A full answer will show understanding of what constitutes a successful portrayal of a character.

4. Identification of moment one carries one mark. Up to three additional marks for the identification of a theatre art, details of how it would be applied and the desired effect.
   Identification of moment two carries one mark. Different theatre art must be used in moment two.

SECTION B

5. (*a*) **Source BofK P.20**
   Tension can be created through:
   - Movement
   - Shock or surprise
   - Silence
   - Action
   - Conflict and confrontation
   - Mystery
   - Relationships and status
   - Threat or pressure
   - Dramatic irony
   or other valid answers, including Theatre Arts.
   (*b*) *Question asks for an explanation of how tension was used, therefore the points listed in (a) require to be expanded upon, or added to with explanation.*
   A full answer will provide an explanation which demonstrates clear understanding of how tension was used.

6. *All words are contained in the BofK.*
   (*a*) Register
   (*b*) Avenue
   (*c*) Strike
   (*d*) Masking
   (*e*) Profile

7. *One mark for any of the following:*
   - Fake blood
   - Foundation
   - Liners
   - Pencils
   - Scarring material
   - Stipple sponge
   - Tooth enamel
   - Crepe hair
   - Latex
   - Nose putty
   - Teeth
   - Wig
   Other words for items such as these are acceptable, if recognised as make-up items.

8. (*a*) *The question clearly states that the scenario must be "suitable for acting out".*
   Scenario
   Imaginative response with dramatic impact, clear plot and strong message.
   Time/Place
   Enables easy understanding of scenario
   Characters/relationships
   Characters and relationships well developed
   (*b*) *Candidates should comment on their desired design concept, not merely list set items and/or costumes. For top marks, a clear design style should emerge.*
   A full answer will describe a clear and effective design concept backed by detailed, imaginative ideas.
   (*c*) One mark for climax, one for justification
   (*d*) *Candidates must show understanding of the requirements of a tableau (BofK vocabulary P.6). "A stage picture, held without movement". Must accord with climax described in (c).*
   A full answer will describe a highly effective and viable tableau with visual impact.
   (*e*) Three marks available for each list item chosen. One mark for details of its application, one for statement on impact. The third mark can be awarded for particularly strong, imaginative and effective ideas.

DRAMA FOUNDATION 2007

SECTION A

1. (a) Clear outline of beginning
   (b) Clear outline of ending

2. **Full name and age:** Both required for one mark
   Occupation: 'None' will not be accepted
   Appearance: Each detail given will gain one mark.
   May include physical appearance and dress style
   Costume: One mark for each idea
   Personal prop: Must match character/appearance

3. (a) *Dramatic part:*
       accept wide definition of 'part'
   (b) *Reason:*
       may refer to plot, characters, impact on audience,
       use of TAs, mood and atmosphere
   (c) *Character:*
       character's role or name acceptable
   (d) *Speech:*
       one mark for each recognisable voice feature
   (e) *Movement:*
       one mark for each recognisable feature of movement
   (f) *Theatre Arts:*
       must match dramatic part stated in (a).
       One mark for way in which TA was used, one mark
       for justification.

SECTION B

4. (a) CSL
   (b) CS
   (c) USR
   (d) DSR
   (e) USL
   (f) USC

5. (a) Name, or role, or purpose in being there acceptable.
       One mark for each character.
   (b) Clear, unambiguous statements for one mark each.
   (c) In each case, one mark for statement, however brief
       (eg brightly) and one mark for logical reason.
   (d) In each case, one mark for statement, however brief
       (eg loudly) and one mark for logical reason.

6. (a) Musical
   (b) Audience
   (c) Costume
   (d) Exit
   (e) Rostra/Rostrum
   (f) Thrust
   (g) Slow motion

DRAMA GENERAL 2007

SECTION A

1. **Time/Place**
   All changes in time/place stated.
   Action
   Plot clearly and **succinctly** summarised.

2. (a) Role: answer must be role, not function or purpose.
       Role may be relationship or occupation.
   (b) Moment: consistent with scenario
   (c) Reason: consistent with the scenario.

3. **Full name and age:** both required for mark
   Occupation: 'None' will not be accepted
   Physical description: One mark for each point made.
   Personality: One mark for each point made.

4. **Relationship**
   A full answer will be well justified, appropriate to
   scenario and refers to the feelings of both characters.

5. In each case, up to two marks available for details of
   how choice would be used and one mark for implicit, or
   stated, result.

6. *Answers must demonstrate understanding of the term by
   matching the voice word to its context.*
   It is not sufficient to say, "Volume when Jo shouted at
   her brother", but "Volume when Jo shouted at her
   brother", or "Volume for when Jo and her brother
   argued" are.

SECTION B

7. (i)   Narrator
    (ii)   Profile (spot)
    (iii) Tone
    (iv)   Balance
    (v)   Venue
    (vi)   Script

8. (a) Names, or role, or both are acceptable. One mark
       per character.
   (b) A full answer will provide a credible, relevant idea.
   (c) A full answer will provid a well-argued case, fully
       backed up with evidence.
   (d) Three marks are available for each section.
       Both characters must be referred to in all answers. Only
       one mark will be awarded if they are not. A full
       answer will contain real detail, a strong idea or will
       show a noteworthy understanding of the term.

9. (a) Theatre in the round.
   (b) Thrust.
   (c) End-on.

10. Hot-seating.
    Voices in the head.
    Writing in role.
    Character cards.

- Named convention.
- How it was used.
- Reason for its use.
- Appropriate context for use.

DRAMA CREDIT
2007

SECTION A

1. (*a*) Full name and age required for mark.
   (*b*) One mark for each valid reason, or three marks for two reasons fully explained.
   Candidates may refer to relationships, impact on audience, mood and atmosphere, characters, plot, purpose/message, catalyst.
   (*c*) Up to two marks will be awarded for each 'other' character's purpose.

2. Candidates may refer to conventions, form, structure, characters, relationships, beginnings/endings, tension, status, mood and atmosphere.
   A full answer will provide a clear identification of purpose/message, with reference to a range of the above features.

3. (*a*) One mark for simple statement, two for fuller explanations.
   (*b*) 'Theatre Arts' implies more than one.
   A full answer will show a clear understanding of how TAs can enhance impact.

SECTION B

4. Two marks for <u>exact</u> BofK definition. One mark for definition which shows clear understanding of term.
   (*a*) Adjustable metal flaps attached to the front of a fresnel spotlight for shaping the beam of light.
   (*b*) Deciding where and when actors will move on stage.
   (*c*) The back wall of the stage, which can be painted or lit.
   (*d*) Rising and falling of the voice in speech.
   (*e*) Sides of a theatre stage.

5. (*a*) No marks; for information only.
   (*b*) Visual information may include set, set furnishings, lighting, set props etc.
   (*c*) Audio information may include music, SFX, silence, etc.
   (*d*) Entrance detail may include reference to any of the naturalistic or stylised movement terms in BofK p.13.
   Reference may also be made to use of characters' costume and/or personal props.
   (*e*) A full answer will include detailed and highly visual ideas that are consistent with responses to (*a*) – (*d*)

6. (*a*) Curtain/tabs.
   (*b*) Entrance/exit.
   (*c*) Window flat.
   (*d*) Rostrum/rostra.
   (*e*) Gauze.
   (*f*) Stairs ("arrows indicate up" not necessary)/treads.

7. One mark will be awarded for each of the following applied to each chosen convention:

DRAMA FOUNDATION 2008

SECTION A

1. Any clearly stated number acceptable

2. (a) A full answer will include a clear outline of the action, including the characters invloved.
   (b) A full answer will give both the idea (one mark) and the justification (one mark).

3. **Full name and age:** Both required for one mark
   Occupation: 'None' will not be accepted
   Appearance: Each detail given will gain one mark.
   May include physical appearance and dress style
   Costume: One mark for each idea

4. (a) *Important moment:*
      accept wide definition of 'moment'
   (b) *Reason:*
      may refer to plot, characters, impact on audience, use of Theatre Arts, mood and atmosphere etc
   (c) *Voice and movement:*
      answer must describe use of voice and/or movement to show emotion, not simply describe the emotion felt, as in eg talk angry, move as if ashamed.

5. Candidates should include:
   • delineation of acting area
   • position of audience
   • entrances/exits
   • viability of the set
   • key

SECTION B

6.
Lighting	Sound	Costume
Gel	Fade in	Jewellery
Fade down		Hats
Blackout		
Flood		

7. (a) Names, roles or both acceptable
   (b) Must be consistent with scenario/characters.
      One mark for each movement idea.
   (c) *What is said:*
      Must be appropriate to scenario and character
   (d) *How it is said:*
      Must be appropriate to scenario and character
   (e) *Movement:*
      Must be consistent with the <u>new</u> information.
      One mark for each movement idea, not emotion
   (f) *What is said:*
      Must be consistent with new information and appropriate to character.
   (g) *How it is said:*
      Must be consistent with new information and appropriate to character.
   (h) *What happens next:*
      Two marks for full idea which refers to both characters and is consistent with previous answers.

8. (a) volume
   (b) gesture
   (c) pace
   (d) facial expression
   (e) accent
   (f) body language

DRAMA GENERAL
2008

SECTION A

1. **Time/Place:**
   All changes in time/place stated
   Action:
   Plot clearly and **succinctly** summarised

2. (*a*) A good answer will provide a full explanation
   (*b*) Make sure that details are for 'that other' character, not own.
   Full name and age: both required for the mark
   Occupation: 'None' will not be accepted
   Physical description: One mark for each point made.
   Personality: One mark for each point made.
   (*c*) Candidate's answer must relate to the relationship stated.
   (*d*) Candidate's answer must relate moment stated, must refer to both characters, and to both voice and movement.

3. Candidate's answers must demonstrate understanding of the theatre art term by matching it to its context. It is not sufficient to say "Stage make-up when the man came in", but "Stage make-up when the man came in bleeding" is.

4. One mark for stated venue. One mark for target audience. One mark for justification of either or both.

SECTION B

5. (*a*) proscenium arch/Prosc. Arch/proscenium
   (*b*) tone
   (*c*) voices in the head
   (*d*) dialogue
   (*e*) hot seating
   (*f*) spontaneous improvisation

6. *Any five from:*
   - delineation of acting area (accept drawing of shape)
   - position of audience
   - entrances/exits
   - viability of the set
   - indication of scale
   - key

7. *Any three from:*
   - communicate a message
   - entertain
   - tell a story
   - educate
   - explore a theme or issue
   - explore and experience (eg through audience participation, forum theatre)

8. (*a*) *Movements may include naturalistic and/or stylised movements listed in the Body of Knowledge as:*
   - body language

- facial expression
- gesture
- eye contact
- posture
- use of space
- balance
- speed
- timing
- positioning
- use of levels
- rhythm
- stance
- use of direction

   (*b*) Candidate's answer should include reference to at least two Theatre Arts.

DRAMA CREDIT 2008

SECTION A

1. (a) Strength may lie in, eg plot, TAs, impact on audience, preparedness for presentation, acting, organisation etc.
   (b) *Any one of following responses which shows explicit or implicit understanding of the drama process, outlined in the Body of Knowledge as:*
      - responding to stimulus
      - offering ideas
      - discussing and selecting ideas for situation and roles
      - agreeing form, structure and devices (conventions)
      - setting up space
      - rehearsing
      - reviewing
      - adding Theatre Arts
      - presenting to an audience
      - evaluating.

      Other aspects may be included too, such as team work, problem solving, attendance, effort etc.
   (c) One mark for simple or single reason. Two marks for second reason. A good answer will provide a fuller explanation.

2. (a) Weakness may lie in, eg plot, TAs, impact on audience, preparedness for presentation, acting, organisation etc.
   (b) *Any one of following responses which shows explicit or implicit understanding of the drama process, outlined in the Body of Knowledge as:*
      - responding to stimulus
      - offering ideas
      - discussing and selecting ideas for situation and roles
      - agreeing form, structure and devices (conventions)
      - setting up space
      - rehearsing
      - reviewing
      - adding theatre arts
      - presenting to an audience
      - evaluating.

      Other aspects may be included too, such as team work, problem solving, attendance, effort etc.
   (c) One mark for simple or single reason. Two marks for second reason. A good answer will provide a fuller explanation.

3. (a) No mark for selection of characters.
   (b) 'Describing' implies justifying, so credit this. Two marks will be awarded for a fuller response.
   (c) Candidate's answer may refer to use of voice, naturalistic and stylised movement and Theatre Arts. One mark will be awarded for each aspect mentioned.

   (d) Candidate's response should clearly demonstrate feelings towards other character, showing insight and depth.

SECTION B

4. (a) and (b)
      General appearance may include reference to make-up, style of dress, accessories, colour schemes, materials, fashion sense, price, sources/brands etc. There is no need to answer 'costume' and 'general appearance' separately. Candidates' answers should go beyond a list of items of costume or make-up details.

5. (a) Candidates may include standard character card details such as name, age, occupation, personality, appearance, relationships, hobbies/interests etc.
   (b) *Techniques listed in the Body of Knowledge are:*
      - character cards
      - improvisation
      - role-play
      - hot seating
      - voices in the head
      - writing in role
      - thought tracking
      - thought tunnel.
   (c) One mark will be awarded for each valid point made about how the chosen technique helped develop a better understanding of the character.

6. (a) playwright
   (b) wings
   (c) dramatic irony
   (d) intonation
   (e) truck
   (f) rake
   (g) gobo
   (h) pyrotechnics (accept pyros).

7. (a) Candidate's answer must match the stated mood and atmosphere.
      Set, set dressings, colours and set props should all consistently match the stated mood and atmosphere in a highly visual, detailed, well thought out and atmospheric set.
   (b) Candidate's answer may include notes on any three or more from:
      - advice on voice
      - delivery of lines
      - timing
      - movement
      - actions and reactions
      - costume
      - props
      - make-up

   NB - 'notes' means that full sentences are not required. Bullet points or phrases are permissible

DRAMA FOUNDATION 2009

SECTION A

1. Time/place not required.
   Three marks for clear outline of action, giving characters involved.

2. One mark each for any five of possible six below:
   • the acting area is delineated
   • position of audience is shown
   • entrances/exits are given
   • the set is viable
   • indication of scale
   • key

3. One mark for one TA idea. Two marks for more than one TA idea, for a fully explained answer or one which contains good use of TA vocabulary.

   Justification not required.

4. **Name and age:**   <u>Full</u> name <u>and</u> age required.
   Occupation: Do not accept 'none'.
   Appearance: One mark for each detail. May include physical appearance and dress style.

5. (a) Wide definition of 'part' is acceptable.

   (b) May refer to plot, characters, impact on audience, use of TAs, mood and atmosphere etc.

   (c) Name or role or both.

   (d) One mark for each explained voice term, ie not just 'I used volume and pace'.

   (e) As above for movement.

6. One mark for explicit or implicit identification of part of process.
   One mark for reason for difficulty. The process is outlined in the Body of Knowledge (B of K) as:
   • responding to stimulus
   • offering ideas
   • discussing and selecting ideas for situation and roles
   • agreeing form, structure and devices (conventions)
   • setting up space
   • rehearsing
   • reviewing
   • adding theatre arts
   • presenting to an audience
   • evaluating

   Other aspects may be included too, such as team work, problem solving, attendance, effort etc.

SECTION B

7. One mark for each appropriate prop and costume idea.

8. (a) One mark for each suitable movement idea.

   (b) One mark for one appropriate idea.

   (c) One mark for each appropriate idea about delivery of line.

   (d) – (f) As above

9. (a) rehearsal

   (b) monologue

   (c) flood

   (d) rostra

   (e) enter

   (f) tension

   (g) pace

SECTION A

1. Time/Place

All changes in time/place stated.

Action

Plot clearly and **succinctly** summarised.

2. (*a*) One mark for clearly identified 'aspect'.
May refer to plot, characters, relationships, TAs, casting etc.

(*b*) One mark for each acceptable reason.

3. (*a*) Full name required. Role must be relationship or occupation.

(*b*) In each case, one mark for audience response, one for reason.

4. (*a*) <u>Full</u> name <u>and</u> age required for mark.

One mark for each personality trait.

(*b*) All three TAs must be referred to. Extra mark for any additional TA idea. If there is a clear link to 4 (*a*), personality.

(*c*) One mark for each behaviour consistent with (*a*) and (*b*).
The reaction must be linked to a voice and movement term: it is not enough to describe only the character's emotional reaction.
eg 'I would be shy and quiet' is not acceptable.
'I would talk quietly and make no eye contact' is acceptable.

SECTION B

5. (*a*) Status

(*b*) Wash

(*c*) Plot

(*d*) Fresnel (spot)

6. (*a*) In each case, for two marks, answer must contain two ideas. No justification required.

(*b*) As above

7. (*a*) Pantomime

(*b*) Musical

(*c*) Monologue

(*d*) Dance Drama

(*e*) Comedy

(*f*) Play

8. • Target Audience — A specific group of people at whom a drama is aimed.

• Venue — Place where a drama is presented.

• Voice-over — Recorded speech played during a drama.

• Hot-seating — Questioning a character in role.

DRAMA CREDIT
2009

SECTION A

1. One mark for each appropriate response.
   "Effectiveness" may be implied or stated.
   Candidates may refer to any aspect of the sequencing of time, time changes, setting(s) and events.

2. (a) One mark for climax. Additional two for full, 1 for less detailed justification.

   (b) All three acting techniques must be referred to.

3. All four TAs must be referred to.

SECTION B

4. (a) apron

   (b) blacks

   (c) cyclorama

   (d) wings

   (e) auditorium

   (f) stalls
   balcony
   (dress) circle

5. One mark for each requirement for each character.

6. (a) 'Motivation' refers to reasons why the characters move in the manner described in the answer.

   Full, detailed and highly visual ideas, consistently or occasionally very imaginative. Candidate's motivation ideas show insight into how tension can be created through movement.

   (b) One mark for each costume idea which is "unusual", defined as "strange, odd, curious, extraordinary, abnormal, remarkable, bizarre, atypical and uncommon".

   (c) One mark for each individual make-up idea or three to four marks for description of clear and effective concept which is entirely consistent with 6 (a) and 6 (b).

   (d) One mark for choice of special effect.

   Up to two marks for the ways in which it would be used.

   Up to two marks for the desired effect.

7. One mark for each statement about what made the drama successful. Candidates may refer to: language and voice, movement, characterisation, purpose, form and structure, mood and atmosphere, theatre arts, acting/reacting, plot, effect on audience etc.

DRAMA FOUNDATION
2010

SECTION A

1. (a) Wide definition of 'scene' acceptable.

   (b) One mark for muddled description, two for clear outline of section of plot.

   (c) One mark for single justification, two for two reasons or one more fully justified.

   (d) One mark for lighting idea, one for reason.

   (e) One mark for sound idea, one for reason.

2. (a) Full name and age required for mark.

   (b) 'None' will not be credited.

   (c) One mark for identified part, one for reason.

   (d) One mark for each voice idea.

   (e) One mark for each movement idea.

3. (a) One mark for costume idea, one for reason

   (b) One mark for personal props idea, one for reason

SECTION B

4. Alternatives to the following will not be accepted:
   • accent
   • body language
   • gesture
   • volume
   • facial expression
   • pace

5. (a) One mark for single or simple idea. Two marks for two ideas or one more fully described.

   (b) One mark for each suggested gesture.

   (c) One mark for any appropriate sentence

   (d) One mark for each idea on vocal delivery.

   (e) One mark for single or simple idea. Two marks for two ideas or one more fully described.

   (f) One mark for any appropriate sentence.

   (g) One mark for each voice idea.

6. Alternatives to the following will not be accepted:
   • window flat
   • chair
   • sofa
   • door flat
   • rostrum or rostra
   • table
   • entrance/exit.

DRAMA GENERAL 2010

SECTION A

1. **Time/Place**
   All changes in time/place stated.
   Inconsistent detail of time/place.

   Action
   Plot clearly and **succinctly** summarised.
   Plot outline given, but not **succinct** or balanced.
   Muddled plot account, unbalanced/confused.

2. (*a*) Full name and age required for mark.

   (*b*) 'None' is not acceptable.

   (*c*) One mark for each idea: may be physical appearance and/or style of dress.

   (*d*) One mark for idea.

   (*e*) One mark for idea.

   (*f*) One mark for each idea given.
   *Candidates may refer to **evaluative techniques** or may refer to use of **characterisation techniques**. Because the question does not refer to 'characterisation techniques', in which case candidates would be expected to include only those in the BofK, in this response, candidates may also refer to techniques not listed in the BofK eg role on the wall, angel and devil etc.*

   (*g*) For three marks
   Full answer showing understanding of the character's development and/or complexities and/or impact on audience.

   For two marks
   Answer shows some understanding of development/impact.

   For one mark
   Limited answer showing only rudimentary understanding with little analysis or depth.

3. Under the headings 'Voice' and 'Movement', one mark for each idea given.

4. For one mark: single, simple idea

   For two marks: two ideas or 1st idea developed

   For three marks: three ideas or two well explained.

SECTION B

5. Alternatives to the following will not be accepted:
   - monologue
   - mime
   - voice over
   - narration
   - flashback
   - freeze frame.

6. Alternatives to the following will not be accepted:
   - tone
   - emphasis
   - pause
   - clarity/articulation
   - accept any 2 voice words not used, in (a)-(d).

7. One mark for each lighting and sound idea which is appropriate to setting, time of day and mood and atmosphere.

8. Alternatives to the following will not be accepted:

   (*a*) Crossfade

   (*b*) Role

   (*c*) Scenery

   (*d*) Tragedy

   (*e*) Focus

   (*f*) Follow spot

   (*g*) Shading

   (*h*) Posture

DRAMA CREDIT 2010

SECTION A

1. (*a*) *'Part' may be a moment, a scene, the beginning/ending, a build up, a climax/anti-climax, catharsis, an acting performance etc.*

One mark for 'part'. One mark for single justification, two marks for second justification or full explanation of first.

(*b*) One mark for each acting technique, referred to and listed in BofK as movement, pace, pause, silence, voice, eye contact, moves, physical contact, contrast, positioning and timing.

2. For three marks: Clear understanding of how TAs can enhance a drama

For two marks: Some understanding of how TAs can enhance a drama

For one mark: Simple/basic understanding of how TAs can enhance a drama.

3. (*a*) One mark for actual or paraphrased statement of purpose, listed in BofK as: communicate a message, entertain, tell a story, educate, explore a theme or issue, explain and experience (through audience participation, forum theatre).

(*b*) One mark per reference to eg beginning, ending, consequences, build-up, denouement, relationships, changes in time/place.

Although candidates may refer to these aspects through story telling, for a mark, a reference to plot must be identifiable.

4. One mark for each voice and/or movement word referred to in appropriate notes to actors.

Both characters and both voice and movement words must be referred to, in any proportions.

5. (*a*) One mark for end on, theatre in the round, thrust, proscenium arch, avenue, promenade.

(*b*) No mark for choice of staging. One mark for advantage, which may refer to audience, staging, actors, entrances/exits, setting, striking set/changing set etc.

(*c*) No mark for choice of staging. One mark for disadvantage, which may refer to audience, staging, actors, entrances/exits, setting, striking set/changing set etc.

6. One mark for each appropriate sound/SFX and personal prop. Use of the latter <u>must</u> be described eg 'pen' is not credited, but 'nervously clicking pen' is.

Sounds can include those made by characters eg drumming fingers on desk, a sigh etc.

7. For each of the three forms, one mark if there is:
- Implied or stated understanding of the term
- Implied or stated evidence of usage
- Implied or stated effect/impact

8. (*a*) No marks for status: response required for (b).

(*b*) One mark for appropriate placing on set.

One mark for each body language point which reflects status given in (a). Justification is not asked for, so should not be credited.

(*c*) *Candidates may refer to eg clothes (style, condition, colour, value, presentability) hair (style, neatness, cleanliness) face (skin colour, health, clean/unshaven if male, make-up if female).*

For three marks
Clear understanding how costume can reflect status: an overall concept emerges strongly, supported by detail.

For two marks
Some understanding how costume can reflect status: a concept emerges in answer which includes some costume items.

For one mark
Simple/basic understanding how costume can reflect status: vague or basic overall concept emerges, but answer tends to rely on listing costume items.

9. Alternatives to the following will not be accepted:
(*a*) stance
(*b*) dramatic irony
(*c*) prompt copy
(*d*) masking
(*e*) rhythm
(*f*) backcloth
(*g*) playwright
(*h*) blocking
(*i*) rake.

10. Alternatives to the following will not be accepted:
(*a*) G clamp
(*b*) barndoors.

Hey! I've done it

BrightRED
PUBLISHING

© 2010 SQA/Bright Red Publishing Ltd, All Rights Reserved
Published by Bright Red Publishing Ltd, 6 Stafford Street, Edinburgh, EH3 7AU
Tel: 0131 220 5804, Fax: 0131 220 6710, enquiries: sales@brightredpublishing.co.uk,
www.brightredpublishing.co.uk

Official SQA answers to 978-1-84948-086-4
2006-2010

F G C

0700/404

| NATIONAL QUALIFICATIONS 2010 | MONDAY, 24 MAY
F: 9.00 AM – 9.45 AM
G: 10.05 AM – 10.50 AM
C: 11.10 AM – 12.10 PM | DRAMA
STANDARD GRADE
Foundation, General
and Credit Levels
Stimulus Paper |

Study carefully the five stimuli (i), (ii), (iii), (iv) and (v)
before answering the questions in Section A of the
Question Paper.

SA 0700/404 6/9610

STIMULUS (i)

Good News/Bad News

STIMULUS (ii)

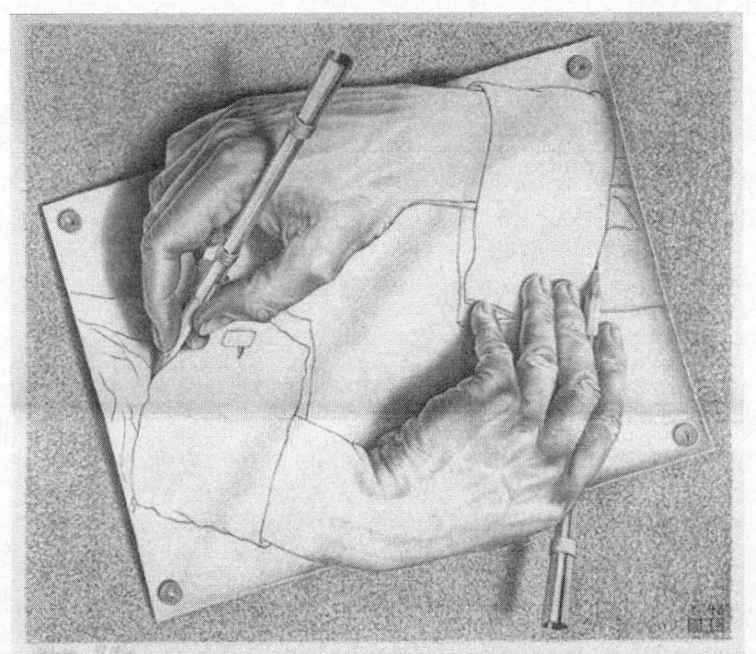

STIMULUS (iii)

I walked slowly up the steps, noticing
the cold damp draught coming from the
opening. I paused, placed one hand on
the handle and, as the years fell away,
I slowly pushed the door.

STIMULUS (iv)

[**Turn over for Stimulus (v) on** *Page four*

STIMULUS (v)

LEISURE

What is this life if, full of care,
We have no time to stand and stare.

No time to stand beneath the boughs
And stare as long as sheep or cows.

No time to see, when woods we pass,
Where squirrels hide their nuts in grass.

No time to see, in broad daylight,
Streams full of stars, like skies at night.

No time to turn at Beauty's glance,
And watch her feet, how they can dance.

No time to wait till her mouth can
Enrich that smile her eyes began.

A poor life this if, full of care,
We have no time to stand and stare.

by Wm. Henry Davies.

[END OF STIMULUS PAPER]

FOR OFFICIAL USE

F

Total

0700/401

NATIONAL
QUALIFICATIONS
2010

MONDAY, 24 MAY
9.00 AM – 9.45 AM

DRAMA
STANDARD GRADE
Foundation Level

Fill in these boxes and read what is printed below.

Full name of centre

Town

Forename(s)

Surname

Date of birth

| Day | Month | Year |
Scottish candidate number

Number of seat

1. Read each question carefully.

2. Attempt **all** questions in **both** sections.

3. You may use sketches and diagrams to illustrate your answers.

4. All answers are to be written in this answer book. If there is not enough space for you to complete your answer to any question, **additional paper** can be obtained from the Invigilator.

5. The Stimuli for Section A are supplied in a separate paper. Check that you have this paper before the examination begins.

6. Before leaving the examination room you must give this book to the Invigilator. If you do not, you may lose all the marks for this paper.

SECTION A

Marks

Answer **all** of the following questions.

> Your answers should be based
> on work from the **stimulus material**.
> (*A copy of the Stimulus Paper is provided.*)

My group chose stimulus _____ (*enter number from Stimulus Paper*).

1. Think of the drama created by your group.

    (*a*) Which scene do you think was the most dramatic?

    _____   1

    (*b*) Describe what happened in that scene.

    _____

    _____

    _____   2

    (*c*) Why was this scene the most dramatic?

    _____

    _____

    _____   2

    (*d*) In what way would you use **lighting** during this dramatic scene?
           Give a reason for your answer.

    _____

    _____

    _____   2

    (*e*) In what way would you use **sound** during this dramatic scene?
           Give a reason for your answer.

    _____

    _____

    _____   2

Marks

2.   Now think about the characters played **by the other people in your group**.

Choose one character (not played by you) and complete the following information.

(*a*)   Full name _____ Age _____   1

(*b*)   Occupation _____   1

(*c*)   Which part of the drama was most important for **that** character?

Give a reason for your answer.

_____

_____

_____   2

(*d*)   How did that character **speak** in that part of the drama?

_____

_____

_____   2

(*e*)   How did that character **move** in that part of the drama?

_____

_____

_____   2

[Turn over

Marks

3.   Imagine all the characters in your drama were in full costume.

Which character would be the most interesting to look at?

Identify that character _____

(*a*)   List **two** items of **costume** for the character you have chosen.

Why would you choose these two items of costume?

Item 1 _____

Reason _____

_____

2

Item 2 _____

Reason _____

_____

2

(*b*)   Now list two **personal props** for the character.

Why would you choose these two personal props?

Item 1 _____

Reason _____

_____

2

Item 2 _____

Reason _____

_____

2

DO NOT
WRITE IN
THIS MARGIN

Marks

SECTION B

Answer **all** of the following questions.

> Your answers should **not** be based
> on work from the **stimulus material**.

4.   Write the correct **voice** or **movement** word(s) in the spaces below.

(*a*)   Way of speaking used in a local area or country.

_____   1

(*b*)   Messages given by the position or movement of the body.

_____   1

(*c*)   Movement of the hand or arm which communicates a meaning or emotion.

_____   1

(*d*)   Loudness or quietness of the voice.

_____   1

(*e*)   Look on face which shows emotion.

_____   1

(*f*)   Speed of speech or movement.

_____   1

[Turn over

Marks

5. Read all parts of question 5 before writing your answer.

> **It is 9.30 pm and raining heavily. John and Mary are waiting for a bus.**

(*a*)   Describe John and Mary's body language.

_____

_____

_____   2

> **John sees a bus approaching.**

(*b*)   Describe **two** gestures that John might use.

_____

_____

_____   2

(*c*)   What might he say?

_____   1

(*d*)   How might he say it?

_____

_____

_____   2

Marks

5.   **(continued)**

| **The bus goes past them without slowing down.** |

(e)   Describe Mary's facial expression.

_____

_____

_____   2

(f)   What might she say?

_____   1

(g)   How might she say it?

_____

_____

_____   2

[Turn over for Question 6 on *Page eight*

Marks

6.   Identify the following ground plan symbols.

Write the correct word in the space next to each symbol.

(a)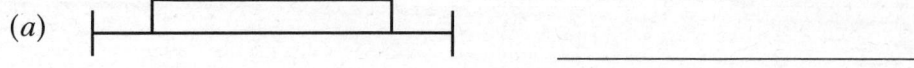
_____

(b)
_____

(c)
_____

(d)
_____

(e)
_____

(f)
_____

(g)
_____

7

[END OF QUESTION PAPER]

FOR OFFICIAL USE

G

Total [ ]

0700/402

NATIONAL
QUALIFICATIONS
2010

MONDAY, 24 MAY
10.05 AM – 10.50 AM

DRAMA
STANDARD GRADE
General Level

Fill in these boxes and read what is printed below.

Full name of centre

Town

Forename(s)

Surname

Date of birth

Day   Month   Year   Scottish candidate number   Number of seat

1. Read each question carefully.

2. Attempt **all** questions in **both** sections.

3. You may use sketches and diagrams to illustrate your answers.

4. All answers are to be written in this answer book. If there is not enough space for you to complete your answer to any question, **additional paper** can be obtained from the Invigilator.

5. The Stimuli for Section A are supplied in a separate paper. Check that you have this paper before the examination begins.

6. Before leaving the examination room you must give this book to the Invigilator. If you do not, you may lose all the marks for this paper.

SECTION A

Answer **all** of the following questions.

Marks

> Your answers should be based
> on work from the **stimulus material**.
> (*A copy of the Stimulus Paper is provided.*)

My group chose stimulus _____ (*enter number from Stimulus Paper*).

1. Use the space below to write a **brief scenario** of the drama created by your group.

Scene number	Time, place and action

6

DO NOT
WRITE IN
THIS MARGIN

Marks

2. Read all parts of Question 2 before you start to write your answers.

Now complete the following information about the character **played by you**.

(a) Name _____ Age _____   1

(b) Occupation _____   1

(c) Appearance _____

_____

_____   2

(d) What was your character's role?

_____   1

(e) What was your character's purpose in the drama?

_____   1

(f) What did you do in rehearsals to help you portray your character more effectively?

_____

_____

_____

_____   3

(g) What would you want the audience to know about your character by the end of the drama?

_____

_____

_____

_____   3

[Turn over

Marks

3. Think again about the character **played by you** in the drama.
How did you speak, move and react when portraying the character?

Voice _____

_____

_____

_____

_____

3

Movement _____

_____

_____

_____

_____

3

Reactions _____

_____

_____

_____

_____

3

4. Imagine you have been asked to present your drama to an audience.
In what ways would you use sound to create mood and atmosphere at the **start** of the drama?

_____

_____

_____

_____

3

DO NOT
WRITE IN
THIS MARGIN

Marks

SECTION B

Answer **all** of the following questions.

> Your answers should **not** be based on work from the
> **stimulus material**.

5. **"Conventions are alternative ways of presenting part or parts of a drama."**

In the list below are **6** conventions. Identify them by ticking (✓) the correct boxes.

monologue   ☐

tension   ☐

mime   ☐

voice-over   ☐

dance drama   ☐

silence   ☐

narration   ☐

musical   ☐

flashback   ☐

forum theatre   ☐

improvisation   ☐

freeze frame   ☐

6

[Turn over

Marks

6. Complete each of the following sentences below by adding the correct **voice** word.

(*a*) Julie was annoyed and spoke with an angry _____ .

1

(*b*) "It's Tuesday", said Iain, stressing the word Tuesday. Iain used
_____ to do this.

1

(*c*) Rachel is nervous. "It was . . . me" she said, leaving a moment of silence.

Rachel used a _____ .

1

(*d*) "I won, not him!" said Calum in a clear voice. Calum used

_____ .

1

(*e*) Name two other voice words, which were **not** answers you gave in (*a*)–(*d*)
above.

1. _____

1

2. _____

1

Marks

7. You have been asked to provide lighting and sound ideas for the following two scene drama.

> **Scene 1 takes place on a sunny afternoon in a busy bank.**
> **Scene 2 takes place at midnight in the vaults under the bank.**
> **Two robbers enter.**

You may use bullet points.

Scene 1   Lighting and Sound ideas

_____

_____

_____

_____

_____

_____

_____

5

Scene 2   Lighting and Sound ideas

_____

_____

_____

_____

_____

_____

_____

5

[Turn over for Question 8 on *Page eight*

Marks

8.   Give the correct drama term for the following definitions.

Write the correct word(s) in the space provided.

(a)   To change from one sound cue to another, with no silence in between.

_____   1

(b)   Part played by an actor / attitude adopted.

_____   1

(c)   Resources used to create the setting where a drama takes place, eg backcloth, flats, rostra, furniture.

_____   1

(d)   A drama about unhappy events with a sad ending.

_____   1

(e)   Key moment, scene, character, relationship or event in a drama.

_____   1

(f)   Powerful profile used to follow actors around the acting area.

_____   1

(g)   In stage make-up, using colours to make areas look shrunken.

_____   1

(h)   Position of the body – how it is held.

_____   1

[END OF QUESTION PAPER]

FOR OFFICIAL USE

C

Total ☐

0700/403

NATIONAL
QUALIFICATIONS
2010

MONDAY, 24 MAY
11.10 AM – 12.10 PM

DRAMA
STANDARD GRADE
Credit Level

Fill in these boxes and read what is printed below.

Full name of centre

Town

Forename(s)

Surname

Date of birth

| Day | Month | Year | | Scottish candidate number | | Number of seat |

1. Read each question carefully.

2. Attempt **all** questions in **both** sections.

3. You may use sketches and diagrams to illustrate your answers.

4. All answers are to be written in this answer book. If there is not enough space for you to complete your answer to any question, **additional paper** can be obtained from the Invigilator.

5. The Stimuli for Section A are supplied in a separate paper. Check that you have this paper before the examination begins.

6. Before leaving the examination room you must give this book to the Invigilator. If you do not, you may lose all the marks for this paper.

Marks

SECTION A

Answer **all** of the following questions.

> Your answers should be based
> on work from the **stimulus material**.
> (*A copy of the Stimulus Paper is provided.*)

My group chose stimulus _____ (*enter number from Stimulus Paper*).

Read parts (*a*) and (*b*) of Question 1 before starting to write your answer.

1. (*a*) Imagine you have to phone a friend about your final presentation. Your mobile phone is running out of credit. Be brief. Say what was the most effective part of the drama.

_____

_____

_____

_____

_____

3

  (*b*) Now, in more detail, explain how acting techniques contributed to the success of this part of the drama.

_____

_____

_____

_____

_____

_____

_____

4

2. Describe how **3** theatre arts could have been used to enhance the part of the drama referred to in 1(*a*).

Theatre art 1 _____

_____

_____

_____

_____

_____

3

Theatre art 2 _____

_____

_____

_____

_____

_____

3

Theatre art 3 _____

_____

_____

_____

_____

_____

3

[Turn over

DO NOT
WRITE IN
THIS
MARGIN

Marks

3.   (*a*) What was the purpose of your drama?

_____

_____

1

(*b*) How did the plot help to communicate this purpose?

_____

_____

_____

_____

_____

_____

3

[Turn over for SECTION B on *Page six*

SECTION B

Answer **all** of the following questions.

> Your answers should **not** be based
> on work from the **stimulus material**.

4. Read the following short script extract and then answer the question on the opposite page.

Pickering:	I am Colonel Pickering. Who are you?
Higgins:	Henry Higgins, author of *Higgins' Universal Alphabet*.
Pickering:	[amazed]: I came from India to meet you!
Higgins:	[with enthusiasm]: I was going to India to meet you!
Pickering:	Higgins!
Higgins:	Pickering! [They shake hands] Where are you staying?
Pickering:	At the Carlton.
Higgins:	No, you're not. You're staying at 27a Wimpole Street. Come with me and we'll have a jaw over supper.

My Fair Lady by Alan Jay Lerner and Frederick Loewe

DO NOT
WRITE IN
THIS
MARGIN

Marks

4.   (continued)

Look at the voice and movement terms listed below.

Select and use any **6** of the terms to make notes for the actors portraying the characters of Higgins and Pickering.

Voice	Movement
Emphasis	Body language
Pitch	Facial expression
Tone	Eye contact
Volume	Posture

_____

_____

_____

_____

_____

_____

_____

_____

_____

_____

_____

_____

_____

6

[Turn over

Marks

5. (*a*) Name **4** types of staging.

1 _____   1

2 _____   1

3 _____   1

4 _____   1

(*b*) Choose **one** type of staging and give an advantage for its use.

_____

_____   1

(*c*) Choose one **other** type of staging and give a disadvantage for its use.

_____

_____   1

DO NOT
WRITE IN
THIS
MARGIN

Marks

6. In a waiting area, candidates who applied for a high powered job are nervously waiting to be told the result of their interviews.

As a director, how would you create tension in this scene through:

Sound(s) and SFX _____

_____

_____

_____

_____

3

Personal props, and how they are used? _____

_____

_____

_____

_____

_____

3

[Turn over

Marks

7.

"Form is the overall style of the drama."

During your Standard Grade course you will have used different drama forms. Select **3 forms** and describe in what ways they were used and why you used them. They need not all come from the same drama.

Form 1 _____

_____

_____

_____

_____

_____

3

Form 2 _____

_____

_____

_____

_____

_____

3

Form 3 _____

_____

_____

_____

_____

_____

3

8. Imagine that **2** teachers are in a room and that they are of different status.

(*a*) What status would you allocate to each teacher?

Teacher 1 _____

Teacher 2 _____

Look at this ground plan of the room.

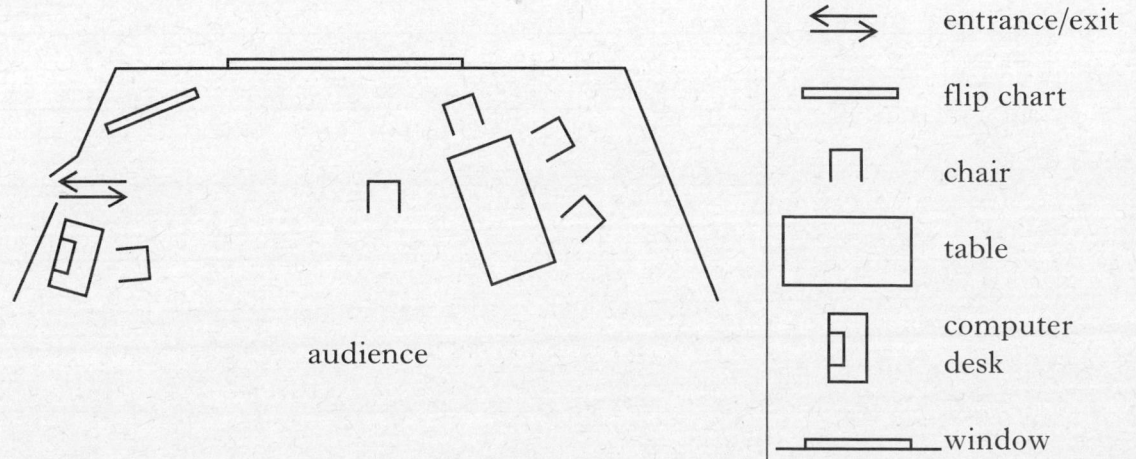

Key:

⇐⇒ entrance/exit

▭ flip chart

⊓ chair

▭ table

▯ computer desk

▭ window

audience

(*b*) Now, place each teacher in a position which reflects their status by writing ① and ② on the ground plan. Then, describe their body language.

_____

_____

_____

_____

_____

_____

_____

_____

_____

_____

6

Marks

8.   (continued)

(c) Next, describe how each teacher's **overall appearance** could reflect their status.

_____

_____

_____

_____

_____

_____

_____

_____

_____

_____

6

Marks

9. Write the correct word after each definition.

(*a*) Attitude or position of the body.

_____ 1

(*b*) Actions or remarks whose significance is not realised by all the characters.

_____ 1

(*c*) Master copy of the script with all moves and technical effects included.

_____ 1

(*d*) One actor unintentionally preventing another from being seen by the audience.

_____ 1

(*e*) Movements which follow a pattern or beat.

_____ 1

(*f*) Canvas cloth which covers the back of the stage: can be painted or lit.

_____ 1

(*g*) Person who has written the play.

_____ 1

(*h*) Deciding where and when actors will move on stage.

_____ 1

(*i*) Slope of stage (to allow actors to be seen).

_____ 1

[Turn over

Marks

10. Look at this diagram and name the **2** parts indicated by the arrows.

(a) _____

(b) _____

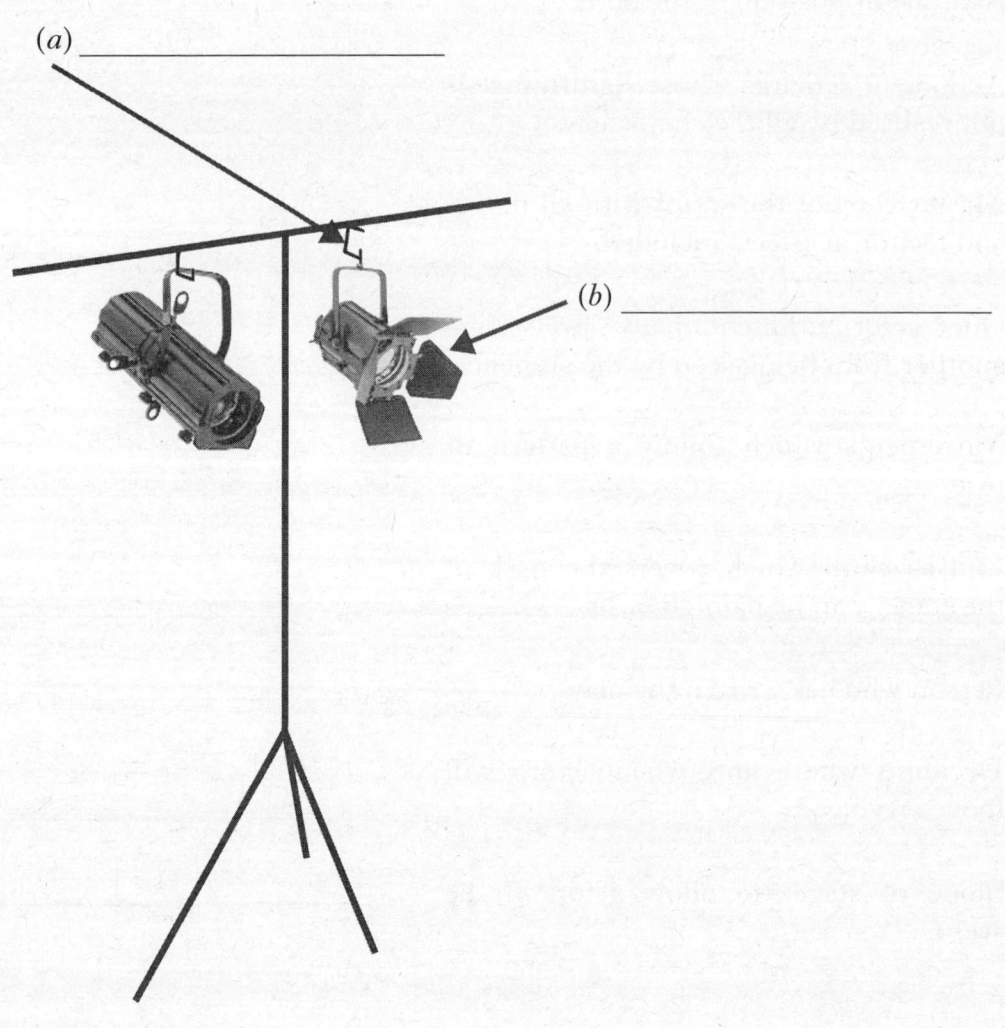

2

[END OF QUESTION PAPER]

[BLANK PAGE]

[BLANK PAGE]

[BLANK PAGE]

[BLANK PAGE]

[BLANK PAGE]

Acknowledgements

Permission has been sought from all relevant copyright holders and Bright Red Publishing is grateful for the use of the following:

An extract from 'Wormwood' by Catherine Czerkawska in 'Scotland Plays: New Scottish Drama' selected by Philip Howard, copyright © 1998 Catherine Czerkawska, reproduced by permission of the publishers, Nick Hern Books Ltd: www.nickhernbooks.co.uk (2006 Foundation/General/Credit Stimulus page 4);

The image 'Flight' by Quint Buchholz © DACS 2010 (2007 Foundation/General/Credit Stimulus page 2);

An extract from the poem 'Flannan Isle' by Wilfred Wilson Gibson, taken from 'Collected Poems'. Published by Macmillan. Reproduced by permission of Pan Macmillan, London, UK. Copyright © Wilfred Wilson Gibson, 2007 (2007 Foundation/General/Credit Stimulus page 3);

An extract from 'Men Should Weep' by Ena Lamont Stewart. Reproduced with permission of Alan Brodie Representation Ltd (2008 Foundation/General/Credit Stimulus page 4);

Extract from 'Iron' by Rona Munro copyright © 2002 Rona Munro, reproduced by permission of the publishers, Nick Hern Books Ltd: www.nickhernbooks.co.uk (2008 Credit page 7);

M.C. Escher's 'Drawing Hands' © 2010 The M.C. Escher Company-Holland. All rights reserved. www.mcescher.com (2010 Foundation/General/Credit Stimulus page 2);

An extract from 'My Fair Lady' by Alan Jay Lerner and Frederick Loewe. Reprinted by permission of The Random House Group Ltd (2010 Credit page 6).